COMPOSTING:

SUSTAINABLE AND LOW-COST TECHNIQUES FOR BEGINNERS

JANET WILSON

ISBN: 978-1-951791-46-9

TINY HOUSE BUILDING CHECKLIST

Get Your Free Checklist:

- Learn How To Build Your Own Tiny House
- Includes Tiny House Plans
- Access to a Private Sustainable Living Community

Visit:
Janetwilson.org

Table of Contents

Introduction

Imagine you are standing under some trees. You could be in a forest, a city park, or your backyard.

Throughout the summer and autumn, leaves and needles fall, and decay, grasses and seasonal wildflowers die.

The rains fall on the fallen leaf litter and forest duff; snowmay cover it. Over the winter season, everything slows or goes dormant: trees, bushes, the roots of the bulbs and wildflowers.

In the spring it warms up, the sunlight increases, and everything comes alive again - including insects and microbes who get to work. While humans focus on the beauty of the bulbs and wildflowers rising again, those insects and microscopic creatures munch away at the fallen dead material. This process is *decomposition*.

Over time, there is a layer on the surface that is dense and dark and rich for the living things. The nutrients soak down through the soil to the roots of the trees and plants.

Let's have a quick look at three layers:

First, the most obvious: The fallen pine needles on the very top

If you rake the top gently, you will find a 2nd layer that consists of darker, smaller pieces:

Under that, is the 3rd layer. A bit of dark soil that is (usually) ½-1" deep.

That is nature's compost. The decomposed plant (and animal) matter that breaks down bringing nourishment to the soil and recycles the dead matter to become a new life. Every ecosystem has its equivalent. Can you see the green shoot in the middle?

Sometimes people are afraid that composting sounds complicated, time-consuming or gross. *None* of these have to be true.

There is a lot of information out there that can be confusing or contradictory because there are many ways to work with the natural decomposition process. You will find that plenty of people will claim that you have to compost in very particular ways.

The fact is, you can *choose* to make composting easy and cheap with simple setup and little maintenance, or you can get into it as an art and a science, or something in between. This Guide will present you with what you *need* to do and what is *optional*. You have choices.

The basic principle is super simple. Rather than being complicated, difficult or time-consuming, it can be rewarding, fun and save you money!

This Guide will give you the information and instructions you need to set up and maintain compost in your home.

PART ONE:
COMPOSTING WITH MICROBES

Chapter One: Understanding Compost
This Chapter includes some Frequently Asked Questions:

- What is Compost?
- What are the benefits?
- Is it a lot of trouble? Is it worth it?
- Is it expensive?
- Will it be smelly?
- How long will it take to have soil?
- Is all compost made the same way?
- Is Homemade compost better than store-bought?

Chapter Two: Getting Started Making Compost
This section gives you the DIY "how-tos"

- What can and cannot go into your compost?
- Different ways to compost cold-warm-hot
- Choosing and setting up your system

Chapter Three: Maintain, Harvest and Store Your Compost
- Maintaining your compost
- Make compost tea along the way
- Troubleshooting
- Harvesting and storing your finished compost

You can use this Guide as an introduction to give you context and help to decide what's best for you, and how to do it. There are step by step instructions to assist you along the way.

Chapter One:
Understanding Compost

What is Compost?

We've described nature's compost. This cycle repeats over decades, centuries, millennia. That dense, fertile dark soil keeps compacting, it becomes topsoil, and eventually is buried deep with the roots as the cycle continues on the surface.

Personally, I don't want to wait decades to get some compost for my flower and vegetable gardens. Are you with me on this?

When we speak of "compost" these days, we are usually talking about some nutrient-rich, alive, dark soil matter that has had enhanced conditions to speed up the decomposition process.

Is Compost the Same Thing as Topsoil?

In a natural environment, compost, (also known as "humus" and "black gold") is that top layer that forms from plant and animal decay. In the park or forest, those leaves that turned to skeletons, pine needles, the twigs, fallen trees that take a century to break down - all of those are gobbled up by insects and microbes and gradually turn into a rich layer of compost, full of nutrients. It functions as both a fertilizer and a mulch.

"Topsoil" is the top 10" of soil. In a forest (or another ecosystem) that does not have human impact, the soil layers have taken decades, even centuries to form. Here, the nutrients and microbial content vary, and it has more air and water retention than the soil lower down. The deeper soil is packed more solidly, less "alive" and has fewer nutrients.

The "compost" that modern humans typically cultivate refers to the intentional use of food scraps and garden waste to make this live, fertile humus that we can add to our gardens.

Topsoil, also known as "loam," is often something that is purchased. It holds a finer texture than packed soil or compost and may or may not be "alive" with microbes. Good topsoil is typically a mix of sand, silt, and clay.

This Guide is focusing on compost that we intentionally cultivate ourselves. When we make compost, we are doing the same thing that nature does; we are just *accelerating* the process so that it doesn't take decades or more to make it.

Compost lives up to its other name, "black gold". It is both highly valuable for your garden and can be expensive to buy at the garden center.

What are the Benefits of Compost?[1] Is it a lot of trouble?

Short answers:
Yes, it's worth it. No, it's not a lot of trouble.

Whether you live in an urban apartment, a suburban home or have a large piece of land, composting will benefit you and the earth.

Benefits of Compost to you:
1. Save money on expensive fertilizers, mulch, soil amendments and liquid plant food.
2. Grow beautiful, healthy plants in your landscape or garden
3. Reduce (or eliminate) the bad smell of your garbage
4. It is one of the most effective ways you can lower your carbon footprint!

Let's look at each of these points:

1. Save money!

The most common use of compost is as a "soil amendment". A soil amendment is a mulch or fertilizer you mix in or place on top of the soil to improve it for growing plants.

If you've ever purchased bags of mulch, fertilizer, compost or liquid plant food, you know that it's not cheap. Your compost and liquid plant food can be free!

2. Use Compost for Landscaping and Gardening

Compost has these effects on plants and soil:

- Chemical properties with plant nutrients (as a fertilizer)
- Physical attributes such as improving water retention (like mulch)
- Beneficial microbes that make the soil healthy and balanced
- The soil enrichment makes the plants stronger to repel pests and diseases.[2]

Another way to use compost that compliments the humus is to make liquid plant food, or "compost tea". Compost tea is the liquid runoff from compost. It's full of nutrients, and you can use it just like you do plant food in the soil. *(See the section on compost tea when we discuss maintaining your compost regarding spraying it on leaves).*

You can make your own
Or
use one of the compost bins that will do this for you.

- Worm bins usually come with a spout so you can collect the "worm tea" which works the same way.

There is more information about making compost tea in the section "Maintain Your Compost" below.

3. Environmental benefits

- The obvious environmental benefit to using organic compost is that you are not using chemical fertilizers that can harm the soil and leach down into the waterways.
- A less known benefit of compost is its power to fight climate change.
- If we are not composting our organic waste, then it is going to the landfill. About ⅓ of the garbage in the US landfills is food scraps. [3]

Why is this a problem? Don't the food scraps rot in the landfill and eventually disappear?[4]

Short answer: Yes (sort of) and No.

Yes, it rots and gets smaller, so it takes much less space than it did when it was thrown away. The problem is what it does *while* it is rotting.

Organic waste in landfills is a problem because when it decomposes in the landfill, it becomes anaerobic. Anaerobic decomposition means that the organic material did not have enough oxygen. It emits a lot of methane and adds to CO_2 emissions in the atmosphere. There are a lot of municipalities who offer industrial composting[5]; these alone are saving almost 9% of organic landfill material and a lot of emissions.

The compost you make at home is "aerobic" meaning there is a balance of oxygen and other factors to ensure that it becomes alive, healthy compost. Anaerobic compost is rotting, smells terrible and is emitting gasses. Healthy aerobic compost barely smells (the scent is often described as "sweet and earthy") and does not give off greenhouse gasses.

Is Composting a Lot of Work?

 Short answer. No.

 Composting is super easy if you want it to be.

In the next section, when we look at the different options for your composting, you can choose which bin or system to use and how much effort you want to put into it. The effort it takes will range from placing food scraps in a small container on your countertop to carefully tending a pile with a compost thermometer.

Is Composting Equipment Expensive?

Short answer: No! In fact, you will save money!

You can purchase all kinds of composting bins if you want, but you can also make excellent household compost in a plastic tub. We will show you how.

Even if you decide to invest in one of the commercial bins discussed, they last a long time, and the cost will be paid back in saved money after a season of gardening.

How long will it take before I have soil for my garden?[6]

Short answer:
Usually, weeks or months but can take a year or more depending on the method you use.

The time it takes to finish all depends on how perfect the conditions are for decomposition. Climate and ratio of different materials in the compost are significant factors in the speed.

14

We will cover all of these below as we talk about the systems you can choose from for composting, but here are some examples of time frames:

An untended pile in your backyard ("cold composting") can take a year or more to start producing compost at the bottom.

Compost in a bin outside can take just a few weeks to months unless the temperature gets too cold or hot.

A compost bucket in your house can take just a few weeks to a couple of months. Again, this depends on how many food scraps you have and the ratio of materials in the bucket.

A compost pile kept at optimal conditions ("hot" composting) can produce compost in weeks.

Is all Compost Made the Same Way?

Not all compost is produced the same way, so you have options! It can be made inside or outside, in a bin or a pile or a pit.

Also, you can choose the amount of effort you want to put into it. It can be super easy,[7]or if you're going to speed up the compost and enjoy the science of it, you can get technical with the details to get the chemical balance just right.

Can I Make Compost Inside without It Being Smelly?

Short Answer: Absolutely.

Compost doesn't smell. Rotting food smells.

This Guide teaches you how to make compost rather than letting your food rot. Compost will *eliminate* a lot of the smell from your garbage as well as flies.

Wherever your compost is, inside or out, when it smells like rotting food, it's because it's starved of oxygen and gone "anaerobic". See the Appendix, "The Essential Science of Compost" if you want to learn about how the aerobic and anaerobic processes work.

How do I Make Compost?

Short answer:
- Nature makes compost through the decay of dead things.
- You make compost by putting your plant food scraps in an environment where nature will decay your dead things and turn it into compost.

How do I accelerate nature's decomposition process?

Short answer: By creating optimal conditions for the microbes to thrive.

You can speed up the process of decomposition in your compost pile:
- You can intentionally layer in a mix of 1 part "greens" to 2 parts "browns".
  - Greens are fresh: for example, leafy things, grasses and vegetables
  - Browns are dry: such as old dead leaves. We will cover browns and greens in more detail later.

- Keep it moist (not wet) because bacteria and microbes need this to thrive and break down the organic matter.

- Give the microbes air to breathe. Just like us, they need it to survive. Without some air supply, the compost will smell bad and go "anaerobic".
- Air also helps get the right balance of moisture as the first scraps may be pretty wet when they go in.

You might say "Wait! I thought you said this was easy!"

Don't worry, it is.

If you choose to have a large outdoor compost system, you can intentionally keep your compost moist. Just give it a "turn" every week or two with an aerator tool or a pitchfork. You can even regulate the temperature by covering the compost pile in the winter, misting it to cool off in the summer and monitoring it with a compost thermometer.[8]

The great news is that If you don't want to do these things, you don't have to! You will still keep the food and garden scraps out of the landfill and be lowering CO_2 emissions; your compost pile will just take longer to produce compost to spread on your garden. The next section will provide clear instructions for various methods of making compost, but let's start here with some context.

What slows down decomposition?

- Drying out: The forest floor might dry out in summer and autumn. The decomposing process is stopped or slowed temporarily. The same thing happens if your compost pile dries out.
- Not enough air: If it rains a lot and the decaying matter is compressed, there may not be any airflow which will also slow down and change the nature of the decomposition from aerobic to anaerobic. The rotting smell will tell you when that happens.
- Temperature is too hot or too cold: The temperature can go above or below what is ideal for the insects and microbes, thus slowing down the process by months at a time, every year.
- A lack of balance of chemical compounds: this is especially true for particularly nitrogen and carbon.
- If there is too much nitrogen, the microbes can't ingest it all, and you get a pile that smells like ammonia. This imbalance can also "burn" plants.

17

Can I Make Compost in a Place with Very Cold Winters?

Short Answer: Yes.

Composting in cold winters just means that the compost slows or stops. It will pick up again. It's still compost, the microbes have to deal with winters in the natural world. Having said that, there are some things you can do to limit the stress on the microbes and earthworms, therefore increasing your compost success in the spring.
There are instructions on maintaining your compost in the winter in Chapter 3: Maintenance of Your Compost.

Is Homemade Compost Better than Store-Bought Compost?[9]

Short answer: Yes, homemade is better and safer too.

Some people say that using bagged store-bought compost or mixing it with your homemade compost is fine. I'm glad that they've not had a bad experience with it.

Store-bought compost typically contains mostly animal waste. For this reason, it can be a great compliment to your homemade garden and plant scrap compost. There are, however, concerns.

Let's look at:

- Concerns about Commercial Compost
- Options If You Need or Want Store-Bought Compost

Concerns About Store-Bought Compost:

My first concern with bagged commercial compost is common sense. We've discussed the science of compost, so you know that by definition, compost is *alive*. Even when it is "finished" and ready to put on your garden, it is alive with different microorganisms. They can undoubtedly stay alive in a bag, but I wonder about their viability in mass production when shipped then stacked in plastic bags outside a garden center in the full sun. Common sense tells me that this might be fertilizer, but it must be either dead (in which case it's not compost) or anaerobic. It also tends to be much denser, which means that you don't get the aeration in your soil that you do with homemade compost.[10]

My second concern is the number of stories of people who have had bad experiences with store-bought compost and not knowing what's in it. One person said he opened up his store-bought compost and it smelled like diesel! Another person replied, saying he had the same experience, noticed there was no ingredients list and called the company to find out what was in it. The company said, "they buy the stuff on various contracts across the country and had no idea what went into it".[11]

All kinds of things go into industrial compost. It's great that it exists as it plays a significant role in reducing CO_2 emissions. Having said that, it includes animal manures; industrial food waste including meat-processing factories; a very vague category known as "forest products" and even sludge.[12]

Those are the concerns. On the other hand, there are a lot of gardeners who say that they use store-bought compost to supplement their homemade compost. Since it does contain animal manure, it can be an amendment as well as filling in bulk.

Others say that bagged is OK but homemade is better.[13]

You are not alone if you find this confusing! Here are our two best solutions:

Best Solutions If You Need to Purchase Bagged Compost

1) Experiment using "the quack test".
   - The reason there is so much varied opinion and experience is that the product varies.
   - I read an article that made so much sense, he recommended the "quack test".[14]
   - The "quack test" goes like this: "if it looks like a duck, quacks like a duck and smells like a duck, chances are, it's a duck."
   - Purchase one bag of compost, open it and smell it, check the texture and the color.
   - Chances are if this bag looks, smells and feels like good compost, then that batch is good. Buy some and use it!

2) Gardener's Gold Premium Bagged Compost[15]
   If your garden needs more compost than you can produce, this is my favorite option. It is shipped in a bag that will breathe and the makers guarantee the ingredients. It has no animal waste, sludge or industrial waste.

Chapter Two:
Get Started Making Compost

What Can I Put in My Compost?

Short Answer: Plant food scraps, garden waste, paper and a few other things.

Whether you're making a pile or composting in a bin, the principles are the same:

- Mix roughly two parts of the "Browns" to one part of the "Greens" described earlier.
- If you are using an indoor bucket to compost, you can use dirt instead of "browns" depending on which is more available to you. Adjust the ratio if it gets too dry or too wet.
- Make Layers of the browns and greens, or if you are using a small indoor bucket, you can mix the green into the dirt or newspaper scraps or other "brown".

Food
- Bread and grains
- Fruit and Vegetable waste including peelings
- Banana peels
- Potato peels
- Eggshells (squish them first to help the microbes access them)
- Coffee grounds
- Tea Leaves

Garden Waste
- Tree Leaves
- Grass Clippings
- Non-diseased yard waste

- Most living yard waste that does not contain seeds of anything you don't want to spread
- Hay and Straw
- Sawdust
- Pine Needles - green and dry
- Small twigs (if hot composting outdoors, they provide air and will break down) not recommended for cold composting, you may also have undecomposed twigs in your compost if used in warm composting.
- Garden trimmings from bushes
- Chicken manure

Paper
- Coffee filters & paper tea bags
- Newspaper
- Paper without a glossy or coated finish
- Shredded Newspaper
- Paper towels, napkins and tissues
- Shredded cardboard

Other Extras
- Pet Hair
- Human Hair trimmings
- Aquarium Plants
- Wood Ash[16] (not charcoal) - there's no nitrogen in ash so be careful of the ratio. It has other nutrients such as potassium.

Items that take special attention:
- Avocado skins, citrus and banana peels

Avocado skins as well as citrus and banana peels break down much slower than the fresh "greens" and dried "browns" in your compost. [17]
Cut them up into small pieces to help the microbes get to more surface area to work on them.
- If you have a bucket or pile going, bury those pieces in the middle where the compost is the "hottest".

- Make sure they do not comprise more than 1/10 of the material you are putting into your compost at one time.

  - Coffee grounds and tea leaves

These are wonderful compost items; however, be aware of how much of your compost is composed of them. They are highly acidic. Many plants love this, but you don't want to tip the scales in your compost to be *too* acidic. Make sure you don't go over 15-20% of coffee grounds or tea leaves in whatever material you are adding to your compost.

Note: If you have extra coffee grounds that would imbalance your compost, some plants love it when you dump your coffee grounds on top of the soil! Rhododendrons and Azaleas are examples of flowers that thrive with daily coffee grounds. I once had a large rhododendron that thrived so well on my coffee grounds that visitors would routinely recommend I enter it in a contest. All I did was empty my coffee grounds under it every day and give it the right amount of water. If you think you'll have extra coffee grounds, do your research about the plants you have and see if any of them love high acidic conditions.

What not to compost
- Meat, dairy, bones
- Stickers on produce - remove them and send to landfill
- Tea bags that are plastic, not paper
- Items that attract wildlife you don't want
- Glossy or coated paper, magazines, postcards, or coated papers from bank offers and advertisements. I can't compost my bank statements, for example. The gloss or coating comes from a plastic substance; it will not break down and will infuse your compost and future plants with petrochemicals.
- Paper with glue[18]
- Milk cartons
- Noxious or Invasive weeds (the seeds can spread)
- Any plant you don't want to encourage by spreading seeds[19]

- Animal Manure of any kind including cow, pig or horse manure[20]
- Dog or cat waste
- Items that can be harmful or dangerous

Can I compost Poisonous Plants like Belladonna or Poison Oak/Ivy?

Short answer: Yes, with caution. A *lot* of caution and the right equipment. Composting these poisonous plants is really for a more advanced composter. Since many beginners ask the question, here is an explanation.

Compost will completely break down poisons and recycle them as non-toxic compost. It's a miracle.

The challenge is that you need to take great caution *getting these to your compost pile* and tending the pile. Wear gloves when pulling plants like Belladonna, then wash them before their next use.

Poison Oak/Ivy is very "woody" with thick stalks. In addition to being pulled out, it needs to be shredded before putting it into a compost bin. The poison will blast into the air during shredding, so wear not only gloves but an entire biohazard hazmat suit[21] (I'm serious) and industrial level mask so that the poison does not get into your lungs. Breathing this can be fatal. Keep all others, including children and animals, well away *and not downwind of it.* (Remember your neighbors or anyone who may be walking by.)

After poisonous plants (especially poison oak/ivy) have been put into the compost pile, it is a hazard for any pets, livestock or wild animals who might be attracted to your food scraps.

If you can shred it safely, composting poison oak/ivy can be a way to deal with an invasion. If you do, I strongly recommend using a pile dedicated to "hot composting" it as described in the next section. Put it in a securely locked container inaccessible to children and animals, and do not mix food scraps in it.

Can I put Non-Organic Food Scraps in My Compost?

Short Answer: The answer used to be a simple "yes". There's been one important change. I'll give you the information, you decide.

Generally speaking, the process of decomposition is nature's cleanser. One study published in 1999/2000 concluded that pesticides were broken down "moderately well to very well". It also confirmed that there is no reason to believe that there is any danger to our health if we use compost in our gardens made from non-organic food scraps.

Having said that, if you put non-organic food into your compost I would not recommend using the "compost tea" we discussed earlier as a plant food because one of the ways that the microbes deal with the pesticides is to shuttle them off to the liquid runoff. Your compost tea, therefore, may have more concentrated amounts of the herbicides and insecticides than the compost itself.

Another issue is that since the review in 1999/2000, a new chemical has been introduced: Clopyralid. Clopyralid is a herbicide used to keep thistles, dandelions and other plants out of crops.

There were two instances of crop damage in the state of Washington from *compost* that was contaminated with clopyralid.

This chemical does not break down and will be in your compost if you put in food scraps from plants that were grown in soil that was treated with it. There has not been evidence of it being harmful to our bodies, but it may do damage to your garden. Research and testing found that even very low levels are *extremely* toxic to peas,

25

beans, potatoes, tomatoes, eggplant, and flowers in the Compositae family (daisy-like flowers).

The longer answer to this question of non-organic food in your compost:

Microbes are great at disarming chemical compounds. If it were not for this one chemical, I would say that putting non-organic food in your compost is not a problem, just don't use the compost tea as plant food.

Since the formulation and use of clopyralid, I recommend either switching to organic produce or only putting in non-organic scraps from the pea or Compositae family. They won't be using that chemical on those crops! You can also keep up on research to find out 1) whether it is going out of use 2) whether individual large companies have stopped using it or 3) whether there are any particular vegetables that require clopyralid to grow on a large scale.

My own choice is to buy organic.[22]

"Cold" "Warm" and "Hot" Composting:

These methods are described in terms of temperature; they could also be described as a "range of speed" for making compost. How cold or hot your compost is, will determine how fast you will harvest it. You might choose to pay an average amount of attention to your compost, or none at all. If that's the case, it will just take more time to get your compost under your plants.

Cold Composting:
- If you are using backyard space, the easiest way to make compost for your garden or lawn is called "cold composting". This method is simple: collecting your yard waste and plant food scraps, then layering them in a pile or bin in your backyard.

- It's called "cold" composting because you are doing nothing actively to accelerate it. You can just let it go, "set it and forget it".
- Depending on your weather, it will take a year or so to start to get some "humus" to be able to use.
- What about pathogens? People often ask whether cold compost is safe for a vegetable garden. According to Cornell Composting Science and Engineering, the temperature range can be at least 104 degrees F for five days and above 131 degrees for 4 hours during that timeframe. If you've made a cold compost pile, it's a good idea to heat it to this level for five days. This method will leave most of the beneficial microbes but will kill most harmful pathogens.

Hot Composting:[23]

If you want to have compost to use quickly and at more predictable regular intervals, then "hot composting" is a good choice. Even though it requires a bit more attention than cold composting, it can still be very low maintenance.
- It's called "hot" because the temperature is hotter, (therefore decomposition is quicker) and the pile is regulated and regularly tended to ensure you have premium conditions for compost to form.

What are the premium conditions for hot composting? The right balance of:
- Moisture
- Air
- Nitrogen ("greens" such as fresh grass clippings and vegetable scraps are high in nitrogen)
- Carbon ("browns" that are dry such as dried leaves or pine needles or newspaper strips have a lot of carbon).
- Temperature (120-160 degrees F).
- At 141°F to 155°F weed seeds and disease pathogens, die.

A downside of hot composting is that the temperature range will kill microbes. Your compost won't be as "alive" with the beneficial bacteria. You still have the nutrients, and you won't have the weed seeds, but you have to decide whether the seed/pathogen concern and speed are the right trade-offs for lively compost.

Warm Composting:[24]

 Warm composting is the literal "happy medium" for a lot of composters. It does not require the detailed attention of a hot composting pile, but with only a little more work warm composting will produce your humus quicker than a cold compost.
- The ratio to start warm composting is 2-parts browns to 1-part greens.
- Stir it up and give it water till they are blended well.
- Every two weeks stir it if the weather is not extremely wet or dry. Check it in a week if it is. Add browns if it's too wet, greens and water if it's too dry. This method usually takes about 14 weeks to produce compost for your garden.

Choose a System of Composting for Your Home

Now that you have an understanding of cold and hot composting, you are ready to choose the composting system you want to use.

These choices rely heavily on
- where you live, what space you have
- whether you grow things or potted plants to feed,
- and whether your municipality offers industrial composting.

Note: These methods are ordered generally from small to large but bear in mind that they are not mutually exclusive. Depending on the volume of food scraps and garden waste you have, you might combine them.

Countertop and Small Bin Composting:[25]

Small Indoor bin only: 13-$30[26]

There are two ways to do compost with a countertop or indoor bin only:
1. Use a countertop container to collect food scraps for the industrial compost collection provided by your municipality.
2. Make a small compost bin in your kitchen.

Let's look at both of these options:

1) Small Kitchen Compost Bin Used for Municipal Industrial Composting:
- What if you don't grow any plants, but you would like to participate in lowering CO2 emissions? Your municipality might provide industrial composting bins. When I lived in a city, I kept a small stainless-steel compost bin on the kitchen counter lined with bio bags. The hot composting of the industrial process can deal with biodegradable bags.[27] If you have no plants to enjoy your compost, an urban composting system is an easy and powerful way to contribute to lowering CO2 emissions.

- When I was composting in a large city, I was provided with a compost wheelie bin that was emptied every week. I could compost all dairy & meat scraps (including bones) as well as the plant scraps (compare with the list below of what *not* to compost in your composting pile at home). Note that not all municipalities accept meat and dairy scraps.

- As we discussed earlier, the household compost is mixed with industrial compost.[28] This practice seems to work fine for the landscaping of parks and city property but is not ideal as a product for a vegetable garden.

- You can learn more and see photos of industrial composting complexes here. Being able to compost to scale is a great plus; 8.9% of US food scraps are composted in industrial plants. That's quite a lot of organic matter kept out of the landfill and instead, put to good use. I hope that in the future the scientists and engineers responsible for large scale industrial composting will be able to address the concerns we have discussed earlier in the section regarding store-bought compost at the end of Chapter One.
- Note that municipalities vary with their compost protocols. My daughter recently moved to a suburban setting where there is a compost bin, but it is *only* for grass clippings and leaves. They do not allow any food scraps and only empty the wheelie bins every two weeks.

2) A small bucket for composting indoors $6.00-$25.00 (or more for decor buckets).

An indoor bucket is incredibly easy if all you need is a small amount of compost for your plants from your food scraps.

- Get two small buckets, size and shape will depend on your space. One bucket will be active; the other will be holding the compost to let it finish while the other is actively being filled with your food scraps.
- A bucket from a hardware store with a lid is about $6.00.
- Those buckets might be a little tall under a sink, in small spaces (like my mudroom) I love this dog food bin.[29]The lid screws on, it has a handle, and it's only 12x12x12 inches.
  - Use a drill to put a few holes in the lid, around both the sides and the bottom (*Not *on* the bottom, *around* the bottom*). I recommend an electric drill with approximately ¼-½" diameter bit. For this small size, you just need holes around the bottom about 4" apart, a few in the sides and on the lid.

Here's an easy and effective bucket method:[30]
Put torn up strips of newspaper in the bottom, about ¼ full

1. Add in some dirt to bring it to ½ full. You can also use more shredded newspaper or sawdust.
2. Put in your food scraps and mix it into the dirt (or "brown" component)
3. Add in a little water to have it be moist (not wet or soaked)
4. Repeat adding scraps, mixing them in.
5. Add moisture or more "brown" as needed till the bucket is full.
6. When it's full find a place to put it to the side and let it finish composting.
7. Stir it a couple of times a week. If it seems like it's too wet, add some sawdust or dirt (something fine) as a "brown" to bring back the balance. Add a little water if it is dry.
8. Put the second bucket under your sink and start over!

Countertop containers can also be combined with outdoor compost bins so that you have a place to put your scraps while cooking and make fewer trips while keeping your kitchen tidy and clean.

<u>Beware of false claims of mechanical countertop composters.</u>[31]

- Watch out for claims of countertop composters that give you compost for your plants in hours. These are *not* making compost. Read the 1-star reviews. They are $300 dehydrators that use electricity to make your food scraps smaller. They use a lot of power on standby as well. They are not using microbes to make compost. If you use one of these there will be less bulk in the landfill; there *might* be less CO_2, (but maybe not because it gets wet again, and rots). You've also invested a lot of money, used a lot of electricity to get it there, and killed off beneficial microbes, so I am unsure about the environmental benefits.
  - Some reviewers report putting the finished food scraps in their gardens and finding that it molds. That's because the good bacteria is killed. Compost does not contain mold.

31

- As well as using a lot of electricity on standby, it is a fire hazard; it doesn't turn off.
- Reviewers report that it smells like old or "gone off" food cooking when it's running.
- Make sure you research anything with claims to give you compost in hours. Microbes don't work like that, dehydration does.

Outdoor Compost Bins $15-$65:[32]

If you are looking for an easy and inexpensive way to compost an average amount for a family an outdoor bin is an excellent choice. If you have any space at all outside, you can use a small countertop bin for collecting the scraps and place a plastic tub outside for "cooking" the compost.

- You can make a simple compost bin that is covered from pests with either a plastic tub or a galvanized steel trash can with a lid.
- Drill holes for air in the top, sides and a few around the bottom. If you think you need more air and require holes *in* the bottom, then it helps to raise the bin onto bricks to encourage airflow. If you do this, think about where you'll put the bricks for support and drill some holes in between the space.
- Put down a layer of leaves or newspaper at the bottom (about ⅛-¼ full)
- Put in a layer of dirt or "browns" to about ½ full.
- Put in your food scraps and turn them into the dirt/browns, so the wastes are covered.
- Give it a little water to make it moist (not wet). [33]
- Keep adding scraps and repeating the steps of turning them into the dirt and moistening.
- If the compost is in the right temperature range, you'll have compost in 3-4 months.

- Here is an example of the plastic bin with holes drilled in it. [34]$ 15-$20).
- Here is a metal bin for $50-$55 that you can purchase,[35] or use as a model for drilling the holes and making your own.

Wire composting bins[36] DIY can be about $3.00 for the chicken wire. You can purchase wire bins starting at $30.00.

The mechanical aerator described below is $30.00[37] – it is not necessary, but makes turning easier on the back.

Wire composting bins are great for the dried leaves and other "brown" components of your compost. If you are using one to include food scraps as well, make sure that you can open the front to turn the compost, or that it is small enough to be able to aerate with a mechanical aerator quickly with minimal effort. Remember that open compost attracts flies and wildlife.

An excellent use for wire bins is for your autumn leaves or dried grasses combined with a tumbler bin or pallet bin system set up (see below). This way you will have the drier "brown" material, handy to add anytime you need it, in the amounts that you want. It contains the leaves, so they don't blow away when the wind comes up.

You can also build a multiple section wire bin so that you can have
- Materials for composting such as leaves
- Active compost
- Finished compost
This Good Housekeeping Guide is clear and reasonably doable by someone (like me) without building experience.

"Pyramid" aka "Top to Bottom" Bins: $60-$100 plastic, more if wood. DIY can be $100 or more because of materials.

Most of these bins don't look like pyramids. They are a neat and unobtrusive way to compost in a small urban space.

33

You can get them in plastic or wood or make your own if you enjoy building. The plastic ones range from $60-$100. Combine them with a small food scrap bin on your kitchen counter, and it is easy and trouble-free to make your compost.

Here are examples of one pyramid composters. [38]

Note: Some pyramid bins offer aerators as an add-on. Depending on your climate, this may be a good recommendation. The sides of pyramid composters have openings to provide *ventilation* but not *aeration*. Unless you turn your compost manually in the trays, you will not be getting full aeration. This can be fine in a well-made pyramid bin like my favorite I pointed out in footnote 38, but in a very humid climate you may need some extra aeration. Pyramid bins are bigger than the plastic or metal bin tubs described above, so real aeration is essential. Again, read reviews, your climate and nature of your food scraps will influence the need for this. You may be ok without the aerator, but consider your conditions.

Tumbler Bins: $55 - $300

Small tumbler bins are not as compact as pyramid bins but are still an excellent choice for a small urban backyard because:
1. They keep out pests like rats and racoons
2. The sealed container also keeps the heat up, so you get your compost quicker.
3. They are designed to aerate easily by turning them.

Turning also mixes up the "hot" composted material that has a lot of microbial activity with the content that you just added. The result is an evenly distributed, aerated mixture that will produce compost easily and more quickly than a pile or "pyramid".

Here are some options for tumblers. [39]

Tumbler bins are for relatively small amounts of compost. The larger ones quickly get too heavy to turn.

My Dad had a large garden with a lot of leaves and grass clippings, so he purchased a very large tumbler. He ended up donating it to a local community garden. It turns out; he was not the only one to donate a large tumbler bin. Since then, I've found out that large tumblers being "donated" (aka abandoned) to community gardens but then not being used is "a thing".

I recommend no larger than 32 gallons. Be sure to look at and measure the size of the tumbler before you order it - photos can be deceiving, it may be bigger than you think! Also note, the cheaper ones are less sturdy. The handles can break, and the supports are flimsy. A tumbler bin is one item where paying more is worth it. Look at the reviews of any tumbler bin that you choose.

My personal preference for tumblers is one of the dual bin models. One of the common complaints of tumblers is that since you're adding in material all the time, your compost is never done. A dual tumbler solves this issue *and* is easier to turn.
- You build up enough scraps to be ready to let it "cook" and set to compost.
- You allow that to "cook" and start filling the other side.
- When your compost is ready, you empty it and start filling that side while the other side finishes
- Make sure you don't accidentally get a tumbler described as "dual" when it is "dual chambers" only.[40] These require that you turn both sides at once rather than one at a time.

Here are some dual tumblers to have a look at:[41]

Purchasing two small tumblers will also solve the problem of "never finished" compost; they just take more space than the dual tumblers.

35

Stay away from the end to end turning tumblers, even the small ones like these.[42]

You can only turn them when they are about ¼ full; then they get too heavy. The weight of the compost "thuds" from end to end. This means that it is not turning and mixing for the best aeration. This "thudding" means that the stands can be prone to break, and the whole tumbler can tip and fall over and even fall on you when you turn it.

Note for all tumbler bins: The ratio of greens to browns are different for tumbler bins than pyramids or outdoor piles. Bear in mind that the tumbler is sealed more like a plastic bin so there is less chance of evaporation. It will need less water and can't tolerate as much of the soaked material like coffee grounds, tea bags or fruits and vegetables with high water content.

Any finished compost should have the texture of a sponge that has just been squeezed out.

Pallet Bin Composting Cost Range is Free - $200 (+ cost of screws, nails & hinges).

If you have space, a three-bin pallet composting system is
- One for materials such as dry leaves, conifer needles and grasses
- One part is for active composting
- One for the finished compost

Used pallets are offered for free on your local Craig's list as well as regularly at home improvement stores, loading docks, hardware stores and garden centers. Your pallets do not need to be that solid or look good unless that's important to you aesthetically in your space. To compost, free old pallets work great.

I love this photo of a person's first attempt at a three-bin pallet system.

The pallets you will get for free will most likely look like this.

You are *not* likely to get free pallets that look like this:

This amount of space between slats in the first photo is excellent; you can see they are not perfect or new.

To build a three-bin system:

1. Get nine pallets if you want ½ doors on the front, ten if you want full doors.
   If possible, you want them to be the same size (usually about 4'X4"). If your pallets are not all the same size, you can cut some of them.

   Important Information Regarding Safety of Pallets:

   - Look carefully for the logos stamped on the pallets.
   - Pallets with "MB" have been chemically treated with Methyl Bromide. You do not want this leaching into your compost.
   - Pallets that say "HT" are heat-treated and safe for compost.
   - Ensure that in addition to "HT" the pallet says IPPC (International Plant Protection Convention)[43] The IPPC designed standards for wood packaging to prevent the spread of pests and diseases. You can trust that the pallet is heat-treated if the IPPC stamp is on it.
   - The consensus amongst composters is that you should stay away from unstamped pallets because you don't know whether they have been chemically treated. [44]
   - Pick up an extra broken apart pallet if there are missing slats in the others. You can easily plug the spaces by cutting up an old pallet and using the slats on another.

2. Gather your tools and supplies:
   - Electric Drill
   - Handheld wood saw
   - Hinges and hooks and eyes for the doors
   - 6 L-shaped brackets
   - Screwdriver
   - Pliers
     - Box of long screws

38

- Chicken wire is optional, some people recommend it, many say you don't need it. My three-bin pallet system works fine without it.

3. Have a look at this instructional video and diagram:
- Here is the "Garden Ninja" from the UK making a pallet compost system. He gives some proper detailed instructions.[45]
- I also like this simple diagram and instructions from Modern Farmer.

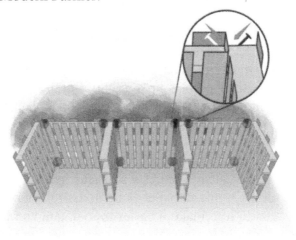

Join the side pallets to the back pallets by driving in two nails at 45-degree angles from the rear of the bin at both top and bottom corners. *Illustration by McKibillo.*

- https://modernfarmer.com/2018/05/how-to-build-a-three-bin-compost-plan/

  That's a great overhead view of where exactly to put in the screws at a 45-degree angle. If you have a moderate amount of building experience, you may not need any other instructions besides this!

- This guide gives instructions for a mixed pallet system with wire mesh. It also offers helpful step by step instructions.[46]

- Notice that when your pallets are lying flat as designed, there is a "top" and a "bottom". The top has more slats; the bottom is for support. When building your three-bin system, you want the *top sides facing in* as they have more slats for support to keep the contents inside.

Recommended "Optional Extras"

- A simple (and cheap) lightweight cover can be useful. Joe Gardener shows one here:
- https://www.youtube.com/watch?v=LRjHZpoPQDY As he notes, this prevents rain from soaking your compost too much as well as keeping in the heat. You can then prop it up for more air just like opening a window. I like having options. It also helps discourage scavenging wildlife.

- Double "barn doors": I also recommend adding hinges to the outside pallet walls and making double "barn doors" out of pallets cut in half. Double doors are worth it to make it easier to maintain and harvest your compost for use while making it harder for wildlife or pets to jump in and make a mess. The "Garden Ninja" above finds that all he needs is ½ door on each section (so 1-½ pallets for doors total).

When your pallet bins are ready you put dry sticks/branches in the bottom, add a layer of browns and start adding your greens followed by brown layers.

If you think you want to "quick-start" your compost pile, you can add "Super-Hot". This is an organic activator filled with nitrogen and micro-organisms. It can also be used as a booster after winter to get your compost going again or whenever you think your compost is not hot enough and needs a little help. We recommend Super-Hot for outdoor pallet bins and piles.[47]

How Do I Make a Compost Pile Without a Bin?

Short answer: Make a pile or dig a hole.

You may have the space and environment where you don't need or want the "middleman" of a compost bin or any container at all - you just want it on or in the ground in your garden. You can do that!

Piles for Different Kinds of Composting

Piles for Food Scraps & Moderate Garden Waste

To start, find a place where you will build your pile. Preferably reasonably level and protected enough from the wind that typical breezes and moderate winds won't blow it away.

Put a layer of dry branches or twigs down on the ground (this will help give it air). They should be ½"- 2" in diameter.

Put a brown layer on top of the twigs first, about 10" high.
Then,
add food scraps and greens on top.
Then,
add another layer of browns on top.
  - This first layer of greens does not need to have twice as many browns on top since there is a thick layer underneath. Just cover the greens well for this setup.

After that, keeping with a 2:1 ration of browns to greens, take your food scraps, put them on top of the pile and cover them with twice the layer of browns.

Most people like to have a pile of "browns" next to their compost pile handy.

When you get enough compost to begin to use, you may want to start a third pile as your active compost so that you can let the first one finish and be easily accessible.

Or

If you have a big backyard or more significant acreage, you might have several different piles for different purposes, possibly mixed in with a pallet bin system for producing and storing compost.

- Leaf Mold[48]
  - Do you have so many deciduous trees that the leaves are overwhelming, and you know that you'll never use them all as browns? You can make a leaf mold pile. Moldy leaves do not have the same nutritional value as other compost, but leaf mold compost improves the soil by boosting the beneficial mycelium and can even be used for planting seeds. It is ok to apply leaf mold compost directly to the soil under your plants.

  - Rake up your leaves into a pile for this purpose

  - Spray water on the pile (unlike your dry pile that you keep for browns in your food scrap compost)
  - If you think they will blow away, put them in a large plastic garbage bag with some holes poked in it and the top tied as loosely as possible.

  - You can keep this as a leaf mold pile, or layer with grass clippings if you have too many of them as well.

  - A leaf mold pile takes no tending apart from making sure they don't blow away and giving the pile a spray.

- Leaf mold piles are breaking down with fungi instead of bacteria, so it will be a couple of years before they are ready to use in your garden.

- Grass Clippings and Cardboard Boxes (or paper)

- Do you have way too many grass clippings to balance with the number of food scraps and browns you have? You can make a grass clipping pile with cardboard boxes or other paper waste.

- Take the tape off of the cardboard if you can (if not, you will have to take it out of the compost when it is finished)
- Lay a flat layer of cardboard at the bottom of the pile and cover it with grass clippings

- To keep the pile going tear/shred your cardboard or paper and mix it in with the grass clippings, then top the layer with some browns.

- Noxious Weed Pile

Non-native invasive weeds such as knap weed require special care, so we don't spread them more by giving their seeds to flourish. Even plants that are native such as certain thistles, mullein or wild mustard will take over whole gardens or open spaces if not managed.

Eradication of noxious weeds is another book, but for the purposes of compost, it is possible to have a weed pile. If you are cutting them when seed can be spread, carry a bag and place the seed head in it after cutting it off in a way that doesn't scatter the seed. The rest of the weed can go in a weed pile.

If you get the weed in the spring before it seeds, then it can just sit out and die in a pile. How you use this pile depends on the thickness of the stalks, etc. I just composted a pile of mullein that was in a pile for 2 years. The stalks were the size of my wrist, so while brittle, they were not yet broken down. I had to shred them, but there were no seeds.

Keeping these in a separate pile and handling them according to the species of weeds that you have is an easy way to stop them from spreading and neutralize their harmful effects.

Direct Composting[49]

Direct Composting is precisely that. Put the food scraps into the ground and plant things in it. Pits or trenches are useful if you want to plant a tree or a row or garden in any shape you want to make it.

Pits or Trenches

1. You dig the hole or trench 12-14" deep.
2. Put a 4" layer of browns in the bottom.
   - The browns *can* be a 2:1 ratio, but they don't have to be. A 1:1 ratio is acceptable because it's in the ground.
3. Put about 4" worth of the garden and plant food scraps of greens
4. *Make sure not to include meat or dairy products*
5. Put the soil that you dug up on top of the organic matter you are composting.
6. Press it down with your foot.
7. Wait a couple of weeks and then plant some seeds or wait longer and plant starts.
8. Direct composting will give your garden a significant nutrient boost.

If you need time to build up enough food scraps to fill the space, then mix in some dug up dirt with the material you've put in and mix it up. Make sure you put heavy rocks or other items on the cover because animals are very attracted to food scraps. You can build up food scraps in your freezer if you want to add more at a time, or just add a few days at a time from a countertop bin.

Direct Composting in a Keyhole Garden

An artful form of direct composting is a "keyhole garden". The keyhole garden is a circular raised bed with a cut out like a slice of pie that allows for easy access to the center. A wire compost bin is kept in the center and maintained with greens and browns. The compost nutrients seep into the soil and nourish the garden when you water the compost.

Keyhole gardens can be gorgeous. Before you use it for your compost plan, think about whether you are prone to wildlife coming in and ruining it.
Here are a lot of great photos, "how-to" instructional guides and videos, check them out![50] In the right conditions after the initial building of the garden, this can be an easy and beautiful way to maintain your compost.

Conclusion of Composting System Options

We have looked at a **lot** of different ways to compost. Be creative with what will meet your needs for finished compost, and what will be convenient.

Remember that you don't have to choose just one!

Here are examples of options:

You might combine a countertop compost bin with any of the outdoor options or with an indoor bucket.
Or
you might do a bit of direct composting for specific areas or planting a tree but keep a compost pile going to produce finished compost for the rest of your garden.

Or

you have a rhododendron that loves your coffee grounds directly on the soil, but you use a pyramid system for your food scraps, and you have a leaf mold pile for the leaves that you can't possibly use up as browns in the compost.

Or

you might have so many grass clippings that they need their separate pile.

You get the idea. What are your compost needs? What kinds of systems make the most sense for your space and what is most convenient?

You can combine any of these systems with worm composting. In Part Two, we will look at the amazing benefits of these wriggly friends.

Once you choose your system and get set up, then it's time to keep it going.

Let's look at how you maintain a compost system as well as the "compost tea" you can make as liquid plant food.

Chapter Three:
Maintain, Harvest and Store Your Compost

Maintain Your Compost

Every household's food, scraps, and garden waste are different. Also, your scraps in the summer may be very different from what you collect over the winter holidays. Moisture content may be up a lot when a guest visits who drinks a lot of tea.

It doesn't take very much work or time to maintain your compost, but it does take a little bit of intention and observation.

Maintenance of Warm and Hot Composting of Food Scraps in Piles or Bins:

As we mentioned earlier, just like us, the microbes need water, air, food, and the right temperature to survive. They will drown in too much water, suffocate without enough air, and become parched and die of thirst if they get too dry.

All of these aspects of balance are easy to manage.

You can tell by looking at your compost if it is too dry or too wet. If it is too wet, it will start to smell like rot. If you are composting outside, then when it's dry, all it takes is a hose with a spray nozzle. Inside a watering can with a sprinkler nozzle is useful. If your compost is too wet, you add "browns" (dry composting material) to the mix and use either a pitchfork to turn it over or an aerator tool to stir it.

For the temperature, you can watch for the steam (which is a good sign of optimal decomposition), or you can purchase a compost thermometer to check and see whether it needs cooling down with some water or covered to help it heat up.

When you are ready to add your greens, keep the layers going with the browns. The browns you add can be dry leaf litter over a pile or stirring in dirt or adding newspaper in your indoor bucket.

Maintain your outdoor or indoor bin composting

Bear in mind that bins get less airflow than outdoor piles or bins. Start with the 2:1 brown to green ratio and see if that works. Use the troubleshooting methods described to get the balance right.

Cold Composting Outside

After setting up your pile or bin with browns and the first layer of greens, continue to layer in approximately a 2:1 ratio and let it work in its own time.

Cold and Severe Winter Maintenance for Various Outdoor Systems:

Outdoor pile or pallet or other open bins:

- If your outdoor pile is 4 X 4 or larger, that helps a lot, in fact, highly recommended if you live in a place with cold winters. [51] The 4 X 4 size ensures that the volume alone will keep it warm enough to protect the beings that are composting for you.

All you have to do is put the scraps in the compost and cover them with a layer of browns that you've saved and set aside to be handy. No aeration or stirring is necessary in these conditions.

As the weather moves from sub-freezing to cycling with intermittent thaws, the scraps will break down. When spring arrives, your microbes and earthworms will have a head start as they wake up and start working for the warmer months.[52]

Outdoor Pyramid, Tumbler or Storage Bins

Pyramid or tumbler bins:
You need to cover these as the compost inside and the bin itself will freeze otherwise. If there is a thaw and refreeze, there will be ice in the bin as well as in the drawers or doors for access. Also, if you don't cover them, you'll have a lot more trouble accessing the moving parts for access when snow covered.

As with the larger piles or bins above, have some browns in a covered pile or bin ready to layer over the food scraps.

You don't need to tumble during a long spate of sub-freezing temperatures, but you need to give it a turn when there is a thaw. Also, be careful that you don't overfill it through the winter months.

Outdoor Storage bin:

This also should be covered to keep it from freezing and allow access to get the lid off easily. Since they are small, it is likely that you will not have enough room for the winter months, so have one or two extra storage bins ready to go.

How to Cover the Bins:

It is possible that your winter is cold enough to need a cover, but not cold enough to be concerned about long solid freezes. In that case, a simple tarp will do until spring after the threat of ice has gone.

In colder places where there are long hard freezes, I've known people who construct a cover from three layers: a tarp, a thick blanket, and another tarp on top.

- I knew one person who used a moving blanket over her tumbler between 2 tarps, and another who attached emergency blankets to a cheap, light blanket. Both worked, and they set them up so that they could shovel a path to the bin and access it easily.

How to Make Compost Tea for Plant Food

"Compost Tea" is the nitrogen-rich liquid runoff that comes from compost. You can either catch it seeping out of your compost or you can easily make it once your compost is finished. It is wonderful plant food.

Catching the compost runoff:

If you *only* want the compost tea without the compost, this countertop bin will give it to you "on tap".

As with any compost, if it starts to smell, add browns and stir it to bring that carbon ratio up and encourage the oxygen hungry microbes to flourish.

You can make compost tea easily with your own compost, here are the steps: [53]
Get a utility bucket with no holes in it.
1.Fill it about ⅓ full with the finished compost. (make sure it is *finished.)*
2.Add unchlorinated water to nearly the top (ratio is ⅓ compost ⅔ water).
3.Let it "steep" for 3-4 days with no lid. Stir it every day.
4.Strain the liquid into another bucket through something like an old T-Shirt or rag.
5.Add water: 10X the amount of the compost tea.
Add more water for young or delicate potted plants so you don't "burn" them

You can store it in an airtight container for 5-6 days. After that, it will need aeration.

Can I use my compost tea to spray on leaves?

Short answer: Maybe.

There is conflicting advice about whether compost tea is safe to spray on plant leaves. I do not believe that you can make a general rule here; it depends on the plant and the tea.

I have had mixed results spraying compost tea on leaves. Once I had houseplants that *loved* the spray on their leaves and garden plants that were "burned". Other garden plants were fine. My roses were ok with one batch of compost tea sprayed on their leaves but curled up and withered with another batch.

If you decide to use compost tea as a spray for leaves, do your research about that particular plant and what it's leaves will like. It might be the perfect thing for some and need serious diluting or not recommended for others.

Understand More Science

If you would like to understand more about how compost works and what nutrients are important, go to Appendix 1: The Essential Science of Compost. This will briefly explain how the bacteria works, the ratios of browns to green in scientific terms and the phases of your composting.

Troubleshooting

The only thing that goes wrong with compost is to do with balance.
- Too dry too wet
- Too hot too cold
- Wrong C:N ratio

51

My compost smells like rotting dead things:
It's gone anaerobic. The aerobes have drowned and the anaerobes have taken over. Stir it up and give it some air and "browns". If it has gone too far you may have to dump it out, clean the container or area (never use bleach, just some soap) and start over.

My compost smells like ammonia:
There is too much nitrogen in it. Add some browns and stir them in.

My compost won't heat up or seems to have stopped decomposing
It probably needs some moisture. Try adding some "greens" and water (but not too much).

My compost is slimy
This is a sign of too much moisture and if it isn't anaerobic already, it will be soon. Add some browns and stir - give it some air. Keep adding browns and stirring them in until it seems to need some greens or moisture again. If it has gone too far you may need to empty the container, clean it with soap and start over.

How to Harvest and Store Your Compost

How do I know when my compost is "finished" and ready to harvest?[54]

Short Answer, look for 4 things:
- When you can't recognize the original components
- It is crumbly, not wet or slimy - remember the "well squeezed out sponge" feeling
- It is dark brown
- It smells like earth (not rotten)

It is important to ensure that your compost is ready to harvest. Compost that is not finished may include chemicals or pathogens that are harmful to the plants in your gardens. Also, as we've noted, decomposition uses both nitrogen and oxygen. If your unfinished compost is under your plants, those elements will be going into the decomposition rather than nourishing your garden.

The reason that we suggest you cut and shred the items in your compost is because it will take sometimes years to break down things like eggshells and some parts of garden trimmings. You should also not be able to recognize the vegetables you put in there, or any paper. Clearly, if you do a little chopping and shredding before you put it in, you are more likely to have a finished compost that looks like "dirt", not plants.

You can use the 4 criteria above for any system - buckets, pyramids, pallets and piles.

In a hot compost pile, you will find that when you turn it, you certainly can't recognize any of the items that were decomposed, and it is not heating up anymore. Separate the hot compost that is finished and leave it a few weeks to "cure".

• By "cure" we mean leave it a few weeks to "cool off". There are beneficial microbes that do not tolerate the higher temperatures, they will be able to move back in and bring their benefits to your plants. Also, you may be lucky and get some hungry earthworms moving in - all the better! To allow for these living organisms and creatures to move back in and thrive, your compost needs to continue to be kept both moist and aerated.

To harvest the compost from a cold compost pile that has not been tended you will need to do some inspection. After a year or more, you might be able to harvest some at the bottom even if you need to pick out some twigs and other larger pieces that have not broken down and throw them into the "active" compost pile.

How to Harvest your Compost:

53

For all compost methods small to large, indoor and outdoor, to harvest it, you just dig it out of the pile or container and use it or store it! Being able to tell when it is finished is key.

Make sure that you've set yourself up for success by deciding when to stop adding materials to your active compost and making another bucket, bin or pile for that while you let your compost "finish". The only system that does not require that you start a new active compost is the pyramid bin system where the compost comes out at the bottom and you just keep adding your material on top.

How to Store your Compost:

Remember, the nature of compost, including finished compost, is that it is *alive*. What we have termed "finished" is when the decomposition process has switched from the aerobes to the mycelium (fungi). It is not as sensitive to temperature, but it does need a certain amount of moisture/air balance to make sure that the living organisms don't die off. Finished compost doesn't need the *level* of attention for moisture and air that active compost does, but it does need some.

It is best to use your compost as soon as possible. It is not topsoil, potting soil or chemical fertilizer. If you need to store it over winter that can take some planning so that it doesn't get too wet and start to rot.

If you only need to store it for a few weeks to months, you can put it in a tub with a little access to air and check it or stir it depending on conditions.

Outdoors, the best way to store your compost is to cover it with a tarp. This way there is some air, earthworms can get in, and it won't get too wet. You can check it to see if it is getting too "hot" under that tarp if it is warm weather.

Conclusion of Part One:
Composting Food Scraps and Garden Waste

Composting your food scraps and garden waste can be an easy and cheap way to
- Save money on fertilizer and plant food
- Benefit your plants
- Lower your carbon footprint

You can decide how much work, time and money you want to put into your composting. You can get started with a rake in a backyard or a utility bucket inside.

In Part Two, we will learn about worm composting. Worms are another way to work with the earth circularly to manage our food waste.

We are a part of nature. One of the many rewards of composting is helping us connect to the cycle of life and natural processes. Instead of our food waste disappearing every week from the smelly bin on the sidewalk, we experience the magic of transformation that literally feeds us as it circles back into our vegetables through our garden soil. To facilitate this process is a connective and rewarding part of life that is both beneficial to the earth and our birthright.

We will now turn our attention to Part Two: Composting with Worms. Here we will learn of more wonders as well as how to make another rich soil amendment that lowers your carbon footprint (and no, it doesn't smell).

Part Two:
Composting with Worms

Chapter One: Understanding Worm Composting

- o   Frequently Asked Questions

Chapter Two: Get Started Vermicomposting

- • How to Get Started
    - o   Choosing a worm bin
    - o   Setting up

Chapter Three: Maintain, Troubleshoot & Harvest your Worm Castings

- o   Maintain
- o   Trouble Shooting
- o   Harvest
- o   Storage

Introduction

Worm composting, also known as "vermicomposting," is an easy way to compost your food scraps and feed your garden or houseplants.

Along the way, we will have a look at some of the science to understand what is going on. We will also look at what the worm castings are.

First, let's get two of the most common questions out of the way, then we'll learn about worm composting:

Chapter One:
Understanding Worm Composting

Are worm bins smelly?

Short Answer: No.

Your worm bin will not smell unless your worms are overfed so they can't keep up with the amount of food scraps and the food starts to rot. This guide will explain how to set up, maintain and troubleshoot your worm bin if needed.

Will the worms get out and crawl around my house or get lost in my garden?

Short Answer: No.

Worm bins are built with lids, so your worms don't escape. If you set up and maintain your worm bin right, they have no reason to want to leave anyway. All they want to do is eat!

Summary: No, you don't have to have a smelly bin, or creepy crawlies roaming around in your house if you do worm composting.

Now that's out of the way, let's learn about worm composting.

What's the difference between worm compost (vermicompost) and compost I make from my greens and browns?

Short answer: Vermicomposting is a different process, and the outcome is different. Worms do your composting to make humus.

Wait, What?

I know, it's confusing. A lot of times, the words "compost" and "humus" are used interchangeably, but they are different. You will see the importance of that difference in a moment.

Compost is the decomposed material that we humans put together from food scraps and yard waste. "Finished" compost has gone into the stage of being worked on by earthworms and fungi. It will turn to humus, but it will take a long time, sometimes years.

Humus is the material that is left when all the stages of microorganisms and earthworms have had their fill. The "compost" from a worm bin is comprised of "worm castings" (aka worm poop) that turns into humus. It is quite different from compost made from food scraps or garden clippings and "browns" in interesting ways with surprising results.

Compost will become humus; after a long time, it is the very last stage of complete decomposition.

Browns/greens compost is based upon heat. You may remember there are three phases:
- a) The primary phase that lasts for a couple of days to a couple of weeks: This phase depends on the size of your compost and weather if applicable.
- b) The secondary phase that is hottest and the most active stage of decomposition.

c) The finishing "cooling" phase that allows the temperature to cool and the fungi *and earthworms* can move in to "finish" your compost.

Vermicomposting goes from "put your food scraps in" to the finishing phase 3 only! The earthworms and mycelium (fungi) in the bin (as well as many other microbes) turn the food scraps directly to humus.[55]

What is the nutritional difference between vermicompost and compost?

When you purchase plant food or fertilizer, you should see a ratio on the packaging that will say 10-10-10- or 5-5-5 or other numbers. This refers to the balance of
Nitrogen (N)
Phosphorus (P)
and
Potassium (K)[56]

Nitrogen
The nitrogen element has come up concerning the C: N ratio. It is part of protein molecules as well as in chlorophyll. Plants turn yellow without enough Nitrogen, and they will also do not grow well without Nitrogen.

Phosphorous
Phosphorous enables the plant to carry energy from one part (like a root or stem) to another (like leaves or flowers).

Potassium
Potassium is needed for the roots and to be able to withstand stress.

Your healthy aerobic compost will naturally provide a balanced nutritional "diet" for your soil and plants.

The micronutrient content of compost varies of course, but generally, food scrap/yard waste compost is about 5-5-5.

The NPK ratio of the humus from worm castings is about 5-5-3.[57] (Please see footnote 3 for a note about the wide range of conflicting information on this subject and the scientific sources used in this guide.)

Is worm composting about the same as compost for my garden?

Short Answer: The measurement of those levels is useful, but not the whole picture. Here is where it gets surprising:

An experiment was done feeding blueberry plants with chemical fertilizer at 10-10-10 NPK, cow manure and worm castings. The worm casting plants were healthier and grew faster. They showed no sign of yellowing and generally thrived much better on the worm castings, including having a higher yield.[58]

It has been established that when you mix in worm compost to comprise 20% of your soil, you will get:
- Better germination
- Faster growth
- Higher yields

Even adding 10% makes a big difference, look at these plants grown as an experiment.[59]

This information is a bit mysterious if you are just looking at the numbers of the NPK chemical compounds, but let's look deeper at other ways that worm castings compare with chemical fertilizer, manure or compost.

1) Since worm castings are essentially humus, the material is better aerated and retains moisture better than compost.
2) This also provides more "binding sites" for the micronutrients, so they don't get washed away. It is a kind of "slow-release" system.[60] Just because there is a number

62

measured in a substance, doesn't mean that the nutrients will be available to the plants.

3) Worm castings have high levels of cytokinin and auxins which promote plant growth.

4) They have higher levels of calcium, magnesium and sulfur.

5) They have 5X more microorganisms as plain soil. [61]
The microorganisms thriving in worm bins include:
- Bacteria
- Molds and Fungi
- Nematodes (who eat bacteria and fungi and make the nutrients
    absorbable by the plants you grow).

6) Vermicomposting quickens the decomposition process by 2-5X. A warm composting method accelerates it by 2-3X. Generally, people report that worms are faster at providing compost they can use than browns and greens composting without worms.[62]

Should I have compost or vermicompost? Which is better?

Short Answer: Ideally, both. Mixing in vermicompost with your compost, topsoil or potting soil is a powerful boost. If you can't do both, look at your plant needs, space and what is most convenient to you.

The pros for worm composting are:
- It's 2-5 times faster. Studies have found that a worm compost produces vermicompost in 4-8 weeks compared to a traditional compost that takes nearly 20 weeks for the same material.[63]
- The worm tea is right there from a spout on most vermicompost bins. Compost tea isn't difficult or complicated, but it does take the extra step of pouring

water over the compost while straining it. With worm tea, you just turn on the tap, mix it with water and use it.
- Vermicompost will not "burn" sensitive plants. You can put your vermicompost directly on the soil of any plant, and it will not hurt it.
- You can spray the worm tea on leaves of plants, unlike compost tea.
- If you need to do indoor composting, it is straightforward.
- If you are composting indoors, you may have more food scraps than a compost bin can decompose. Since worms are faster, they can handle more scraps per week.

The cons of worm composting are:
- Worms can go for six weeks just eating a few cups of scraps and a bunch of paper you've put into your bin. However, if you travel a lot, or make extended trips, you may need to arrange a person to feed your worms food scraps and ensure the moisture content is OK. Also, depending on your climate, the moisture might need a "top-up" to keep your worms healthy.
- If the primary source of your material to compost is garden waste, the worm farm required to compost this volume is more effort in both setup and maintenance than a browns and greens compost pile. Having said that, if you want to have a worm farm with a lot of worms and sell them as a small business, then this may not be a disadvantage to you.

How Do Worms Make Compost?

Short Answer: They eat and excrete.

As mentioned earlier, the worms eat the dirt, paper and food scraps then excrete it. In the worm's gut are massive amounts of microbes which are digesting the material and also excreted with the worm castings.

Remember, the microbes inside the worm's digestive tract include bacteria, fungi, nematodes and protozoa.

The worms need the microbes because they do not have the enzymes to break down the food and absorb the nutrients. The bacteria do most of this work for the worm, and the worm absorbs the nutrients into its bloodstream. [64]

The worm castings are filled with beneficial microbes as well as being fluffy for aeration and able to retain moisture.

What keeps worms happy and quickly eating up my food scraps?

Short Answer: Moisture, food, air, not too much acid.

Why is moisture essential? How do I know it's the right amount of moisture?

Let's look at a little bit of anatomy. Worms don't have lungs. They breathe through their skin. Worms are 75% water. They die if they get dehydrated, and labor harder and slower if they are not breathing well. On the other hand, they can drown. Keeping the bin at a proper moisture level will mean that they are not working so hard to breathe and can be more efficient as they process their food.[65]

The optimal moisture level is 75% - that amounts to a few drops if you pick up their bedding and squeeze it tightly.

How much do worms need to eat?

You want enough food, but not too much or it will go rancid in your worm bin. Your average indoor container has 1-lb. (1000) worms. They can eat about 3-1/2 lbs. of food scraps per week.

How do I make sure they get enough air?

Worms composting bins are made with airflow, and DIY instructions will tell you how to include this feature. As you get started, you can gently lift the bedding and turn it a bit to ensure that the environment is spongy rather than too wet or dense.

Can worm castings burn my plants like some compost?

Short Answer: No[66]

Is it a lot of work to make worm tea for a liquid plant food?

Short Answer: No. If you purchase a bin, your worm tea will come out of a spigot at the bottom. You just add water and use it.

If you make a bin from a plastic tub, you can choose to make holes in the bottom and construct a tray to catch the worm tea.

To make liquid plant food, the ratio is 1-part full strength worm tea to 10-parts water. This method will create a worm tea that is safe and very nourishing for your plants.

Are worms high or low maintenance?

Short Answer: Generally, very low maintenance. There is a bit of a learning curve and attention required, but not a lot of time-consuming or difficult maintenance.

I've had a couple of decades working with worms, and I've found them to be extremely low maintenance. I never had any smell or worm carnage from high/low moisture issues.

I do know a person whose worms died when she started travelling a lot. Even though she lived in a moderate climate, they got too cold in the winter (this could have been easily prevented with a cover on the outdoor bin), and they did not have enough food or water (the amount of travel she was doing would have required someone to feed them).

My first worm bin came from a local waste management program, and I kept it outside the back door in the kitchen. When I set it up, I read instructions carefully and checked on the worms to get a feel of the right moisture content and amount of food. The first week, I weighed the food scraps I was adding. After that, I had a sense of what 3-1/2 lbs were for the week. I also watched to see how long it took them to eat the paper.

After just a week or two of observation, everything was going fine, and after that, I just put in the food scraps, covered them with paper and harvested the worm castings and worm tea. Occasionally I would check the moisture/aeration. In the heat of summer, I might need to add a bit more water.

How do I know when there are too many worms?

Worms double their population every 90 days. Check your worm bin to see the maximum number of worms it will sustain.
- Remember, 1-lb of worms is 1000 worms. Your average bin will hold 1000 worms per square foot, so it's easy to calculate when you will reach your sustainable limit.
- This worm bin[67] If you started with 1,000 worms, then you'd hit 8,000 in 5-1/2 months.
- Bear in mind; you would need to be aware of how many worms you can sustain with your food scraps.
  - 8000 worms would need 20-28 lbs of food scraps per week.

In the past, I have advertised listings on Craig's list a few times to sell or give away worms when they thrived to the point of having too many. You can also put them outside in your garden when the conditions are good for them, the garden, outdoor raised beds and potted plants love them! I can plan ahead and do it at my convenience. We discuss how to harvest worms in Part Two: Chapter Three "Maintain, Harvest and Store your Worm Compost" coming up.

Having said that, other people do report some challenges. We will address those in troubleshooting. Most problems are easily solved with a balance of moisture and air or paper or "browns" and food scraps.

Which worms are best?

Short Answer: Look for "red wiggler" worms. Do not use earthworms.

Red-wiggler worms eat scraps faster and like to be more on the surface of the earth. Earthworms like to burrow deep. They can even kill themselves trying to burrow deeper than the bin at the bottom. [68]

How long do compost worms live?

Short (and only) answer: About a year in a worm bin.[69]

Are worm bins for indoor or outdoor?[70]

Short answer: Either. Which suits you best?

I love having an indoor bin that is compact and easily accessible to the kitchen. I have also had a worm bin outside for years.

An indoor bin might be right for you if:

- You live in an apartment or small house with no back-yard space.
- You love the ease and convenience of it.
- You just want to compost your food scraps.
- You live in a place with winters often colder than 55 degrees or summer temperatures hotter than 80 degrees.

An outdoor bin might be right for you if:
- You want more worms and a more extensive "worm farm" operation for your landscaping.
- You want to include some yard waste in your worm compost.
- You have no room at all inside, but you do have a place outside your back door.
- You live in a place with temperatures usually between 55-77/80 degrees F.

Is worm composting expensive?

Short Answer: No. You can start with a plastic tub for $5.89.[71] A compact worm bin is $80.[72] A pound of red wigglers is about $45.00.

To get started, it will cost you $51-$130 including worms, depending on the worm bin you choose. After that, there does not need to be any cost at all. The amount you will save on plant food and fertilizer will catch up to your original expense. After that, your worms will begin to be a *saving* rather than an expense.

How do I get started with my worm composting?

Short Answer: Get a bin, get some bedding, get some worms and feed them.

The next chapter will show you how.

Chapter Two:
Getting Started

Choosing a Bin and Setting It Up

What are your priorities?

If cost is your priority, you can get a plastic tub for $6.00, drill some holes in the top and start your worm composting.

If ease and convenience is your priority, then spending roughly $80 for a worm bin tower with a worm tea spigot is an excellent option.

Here is a summary of instructions for various bin options:

Plastic Tub[73]

A 5-10-gal plastic tub is usually recommended. One square foot of surface area is needed for each pound of food waste to be added each week.

1. Drill ¼-1/2-inch holes around the top, about three inches apart
   If your bin is outside, you may choose to put holes in the bottom for drainage instead of harvesting worm tea.

2. If you do want to harvest worm tea, you can drill holes in the bottom and set the plastic bin on top of something that can catch the drippings.

3. Add paper bedding.

Get a bunch of newspaper and other non-coated or non-glossy paper and put it through a shredder (not made into confetti, strips) or rip it up to no more than 1-2" wide.

Put the strips into a large bag and add a bit of water. Shake it up and check the moisture. It's important that it not be "wet" or dripping – it should be the amount of moisture of a well squeezed out sponge.

With each handful, you take out you may have to squeeze then separate the strips again (as they will be dense from pressing) put them in the bottom of the tub.

Fill the tub 3/4 full with the moist shredded paper. You want the worms to be able to move through it with ease, so don't pack it. Just set each handful on top carefully till the bin is half full.

4. Add worms! Add 1 pound of worms per square foot of bin. When you add them, lift the bedding, so they get to a lower layer – about 2/3 the way down.

   Place them in handful by handful, a different spot each time. Go up a layer if you've used all the "spots" in the first layer where you started.

Some people say you should lift the bedding to add the chopped-up food scraps, so they are not on top, others just place the food scraps on top then put on the lid. I have always just set mine on top, but you can experiment for yourself.

Wherever you place your food scraps, place a flat sheet of newspaper over the top before you close the lid. This helps keep down fruit flies.

Cinder Block Worm Bin

Outdoor bins can be made larger. Up to 4 feet wide by 3 feet long by 2 feet high. Keep the size manageable and remember that you will need to maintain it and cover it with a tight-fitting lid. You can recycle a barrel, trunk or old drawer, but stacking cinder blocks to the desired size is very easy to do.

If you are using outdoor space in a place with a moderate climate, you can make a simple worm bin from cinder blocks. Decide how many square feet you need for your food scraps and make a square. It's good to start with 3-4 cinder blocks high.

The general consensus amongst worm farmers is that outdoor bins can be 3 feet long by 2 feet high. The key is to build it so that you can make a tight-fitting lid.[74]

This kind of bin only works in places with moderate temperatures. If it gets "a little" too hot or cold, they will burrow into the ground below, but it is not recommended for snowy places or deserts.

Prepare the bedding just as we've described above for the plastic bin and add your worms.

An Indoor Worm "Pyramid" with a Spigot for Worm Tea

Here is an example of an indoor friendly bin with a small footprint (only 16"x16").

https://www.dripworks.com/worm-factory?gclid=Cj0KCQjw-_j1BRDkARIsAJcfmTGg-7VN9CYuCYRJneG6l94T1PWMVWkdJj559kR3J3B3qvmlIRBntoYaAoFmEALw_wcB

There seems to be a lot of customer service issues with the Amazon providers of worm bins. If you decide to purchase a worm tower, I would strongly suggest going to a reputable business directly rather than buying from Amazon. Here are three options that I know are reputable:

- DripWorks (includes a short helpful video too) https://www.dripworks.com/worm-factory?gclid=Cj0KCQjw-_j1BRDkARIsAJcfmTGg-7VN9CYuCYRJneG6l94T1PWMVWkdJj559kR3J3B3qvmlIRBntoYaAoFmEALw_wcB

- Uncle Jim's Worm Farm
- https://unclejimswormfarm.com/order-stuff/indoor-compost-bin/
  - o Tip: I also like Uncle Jim's Worm Blanket
  - o https://unclejimswormfarm.com/product/supplies/worm-blanket/

- Gardeners Supply (check out their customer guarantee) https://www.gardeners.com/search?q=worm+composter&simplesearch=submit#q=worm%20composter

All of these companies mentioned have solid reputations for customer service if you need it, and you can contact them with questions as well.

A "Flow-Through" Worm Bin System

I see this kind of system a kind of a mix between a plastic tub and a pyramid bin. It is layered like a tub; there is one container, not trays. Often these bins look like funnels that are hanging on a frame. The worm tea drips out of the bottom, and you harvest the worm castings from the bottom.

Here is an example:
https://www.amazon.com/gp/product/B01CRJGUOG/ref=as_li_tl?imprToken=Itdp81VxCoiMoU5j376LTg&slotNum=9&ie=UTF8&tag=backyardboss-

Here is an attractive, modern-looking flow-through system that has reliable reviews. It is less of a funnel shape but still a flow-through system.
https://www.amazon.com/dp/B078RHPWZ4/ref=dp_prsubs_1

Some people swear by flow-through bins and say that they have fewer un-composted pieces and worms in the bottom when they harvest the castings. Others have found that the funnel shape does not have enough drainage. If you like this idea, I would recommend one like the Urban Worm Bag that does not have such a dramatic funnel angle at the bottom.

Setting Up Any Worm Bin

For any bin, once you have set it up and have the worms tucked in the bedding, put about 4 cups of food scraps on top of the bedding, add another layer of bedding on top and a solid sheet of newspaper or a worm blanket, and let them work on it for a few days. You will quickly get a feel for how much they eat.

What do they eat? In Chapter Three, we will look at the foods you can and can't put in, and how to maintain your bin. We will also discuss harvesting and storing your worm castings.

Chapter Three:
Maintain, Harvest & Store Your Worm Castings

What Can and Can't Go into My Worm Bin?

Below you will find three lists:
- What your worms love
- What is not good for them
- Items that can go in with some special attention

Like compost piles or buckets, you still need to be aware of balance. Basic principles and common sense do not take time or effort, just awareness.

For example, yes you can put in tea bags and coffee grounds, but these items are acidic, so if you put in too many compared to your food scraps your worms will not get the right nutrition and will get literally burned on their skin from the imbalance. This is why there is the list of items that can go into your worm bin but need special consideration.

What is Good for Your Worms

Vegetables

Non-citrus fruit including rinds of melons and banana peels

Tea and tea bags (you can put in the string and the paper tag!)

Used paper towels if not greasy or have chemicals on them.

Egg cartons (remove any stickers or labels and cut into pieces)
Coffee grounds and unbleached filters mixed in with other scraps –
careful not to get too much, so the overall balance does not get too
acidic

- Fun fact: worms love coffee so much that it is used to *attract* them! [75]

Crushed eggshells. It takes longer for them to break down, but
they are suitable for your worms so crush them to help the worms
out.

What is Not Good for Your Worms

Meat and Dairy*[76]

Oils and High Fat Foods (the bedding can become greasy so the
worms can't breathe) *
    Peanut butter is an example.

Bread (sucks up moisture, becomes dense and is prone to mold
quickly)

Raw Onions and Garlic

Citrus

Spicy foods such as hot peppers or sauces with a lot of pepper
(Worms avoid them, and it can burn their skin.)

Paper that has a glossy or coated finish (like magazines and most
mailed fliers)

Bleached white office paper (unbleached is fine)

Yard trimmings that have been treated with pesticides.

Poison ivy, oak or sumac or other poisonous plants

76

Plants that are invasive weeds such as knapweed – the seeds will get a boost for germination, and you will spread the weeds wherever the compost goes.

Plastic, metals, glass or other non-biodegradable items. This includes some tea bags that are plastic mesh.

Yes, but with Special Care:

Grass clippings – too many will make the bin overly rich in Nitrogen, and the bin will heat up too much. A little bit is OK.

Canned Sauces, other processed food These items are often salty (not good for worms) or fatty (also not good for them). You may also find that there are chemicals, including pesticides in them.
Coffee Grounds

- As mentioned earlier, worms *love* coffee grounds, but because they are acidic, you don't want to get too much.

- Add them mixed in with other food scraps (never alone)
  - The coffee grounds should not be more than 1/3 of the offering at most. Think about the common sense of a balanced diet.

- You will know there is too much coffee or other acidic material if your bin smells like vinegar.

Citrus & peels

- Worms don't like citrus that much. Also, the peels take a long time to break down (they need to be cut up into pieces), and *citrus is acidic*. Cutting up and tossing in the occasional orange peel with other food scraps, for example, is fine. However, they should not be a part of their regular diet, and certainly not without other food scraps. Don't put in very much at a time.

Tomatoes and Tomato Sauces

Again, acid is the issue. Scraping off a bit of spaghetti sauce off a plate when it's going into a mix with vegetables is okay every once in a while; but not a dish full of spaghetti sauce from the kid who didn't eat their dinner. Also, don't pour in a lot of leftover sauce.

Avocado peels

Avocado peels take much longer to break down than your vegetables like lettuce or zucchini. They even take longer than eggshells. If you put one in your worm bin once in a while, chop it up as fine as you can. Then there is a lot of surface area for the worm and the microorganisms to work with.

Can I feed my worms too much or can they handle as much as the bin will hold?

Short Answer: Yes. You can feed them too much, and it will kill them.

The food will start to go anaerobic, and the worms will want to move out. If they can't get out, they will die.

This is why it is good to feed a pound of worms about 4 cups of food scraps with bedding on top to get started. After that, look at it in a couple of days and see how much is eaten. Soon you will know how often your worms go through your food scraps so that you won't overwhelm them.

Tips for Maintaining your Worm Bin[77]

When you feed your worms, take a moment to gently lift the bedding in a few places before adding the scraps. This is a super-easy way to aerate the bin, and you are also checking to make sure your worms have the right amount of moisture.

If you are keeping your worm bin in a basement or garage, make sure that the temperature range will be between 50-75/80.

Chop up your vegetable bits into approx. 1" pieces. Don't put them in a blender as this will degrade quicker, and the worms will not be able to eat it before it rots.

If you mix a little bit of bedding into the food before you add it, the food is aerated and all the more attractive and edible to your worms.

I love having these three tools:

A temperature thermometer https://www.amazon.com/Worm-Farming-Thermometer-Wiggler-Compost/dp/B00SKJ8OAG/ref=sr_1_5?dchild=1&keywords=worm+composting+bin+accessories&qid=1589816619&s=lawn-garden&sr=1-5

A PH meter: https://www.amazon.com/Worm-Farming-Meter-Wiggler-Composting/dp/B00SNHUZ6G/ref=sr_1_8?dchild=1&keywords=worm+composting+bin+accessories&qid=1589816619&s=lawn-garden&sr=1-8

A Moisture meter: https://www.amazon.com/Farming-Moisture-Meter-Wiggler-Composting/dp/B00SNHEGKW/ref=sr_1_9?dchild=1&keywords=worm+composting+bin+accessories&qid=1589816619&s=lawn-garden&sr=1-9

These can be useful for compost as well, of course. As a beginner, the measurement helps you. It tells you whether there was too much acid in your food scraps or too much or too little moisture. They are not necessary; most people don't use them and do fine. Having said that, they make composting even more manageable, and they are beneficial when you are getting started.

Can I keep worms outside in the winter?

There are worm bins that are made to withstand more extreme temperatures; the challenge is keeping the worms happy.

It is vital for the bin to be in a shady spot, never in direct sunlight.

As we have discussed, the temperature range for happy worms is 55-75 degrees. They will slow down at the outer edges of the spectrum, and certainly above or below them. They can tolerate down to 50 and up to 80 for days here and there or a week or so. Temperatures over 85 or under 40 degrees will kill them.

If you live in a place where it is not likely to be outside 55-75 degrees generally, then it is easy to cover the bin to keep it warm for a day or two in a cold snap and bring it inside if it is over 75 degrees in the shade.

I kept a worm bin outside in a city in a warm climate for decades. There were days here and there or even a week or two when I covered my bin or brought it inside. I did have access to deep shade that was very rarely over 75 even when the temperatures were in the 90's. When it was cold, and the temps dipped below 55, I just covered it, and also though they slowed down a bit, they were safe and got back up to speed as soon as it was not so cold.
Now I live on a mountain at 4000 feet, and my worms are happily inside the kitchen in a smaller worm bin. Winters here are long and cold, trying to keep a worm bin outside would involve some kind of heating system. I would also have to shovel snow in order to add food scraps to my worm bin.

Think about your climate, convenience, what will make this easy and makes sense for you.

Troubleshooting Worm Bins

Worm Bin Smells Like Rot

Rot is a sign that the scraps have become anaerobic. This is a toxic environment for your worms.

Check on these things:[78]

- Are the worms overfed? Did they eat up the last food scraps?

- Is the bin too wet?
    If so, add more bedding and lift the layers to aerate. Do this every day until the problem is eradicated.

- Don't add melons or other foods with a lot of moisture content until the problem balances out. After that, be aware of the ratio of high vs less moisture content foods.
- Were there any meat, bones, dairy or oils in the food scraps? As mentioned above in what not to give your worms, these things break down much slower and will go rotten before the worms can eat them.

Worm Bin Smells Like Vinegar

The vinegar smell means the bin is becoming too acidic. You might be adding too many coffee grounds or other acidic foods. You may have been perfectly fine, adding a certain amount of coffee grounds, but then had a couple of meals that included a lot of tomato-based foods and the two together tipped the balance of your bin.

What is pH balance, and how does it work in my worm bin?

The scale of pH is between 0-14. It refers to the balance of acid and alkaline.

- 7 is neutral
- The pH of your worm bin should be 6-7[79]

To restore the pH balance for your worms.

- Add some bedding
- Ensure that there are no acidic food scraps left uneaten
- Ensure that there is not too much food

Also, check the general moisture level. When problems arise, it isn't necessarily just one thing that is causing it. Lift up the layers to aerate and check that the moisture level of the bin is right.

Worms Do Not Move Up to the Top Tray or Layer of My Bin

- This is your worms telling you that for some reason, they are getting what they need in the deeper layers where they are and that the top is not as appealing.

- Make sure that there are no uneaten scraps in the lower layers. If they don't show signs of rotting, move the scraps back up to the top, so there is no food in the lower layers of worm castings.

- How is the moisture level on top? Is there yummy food that they like? Attract them with a few coffee grounds.

- Is the top layer dark enough? Worms hate light. Even with a lid, sometimes aeration holes or just the plastic of a bin can let in enough light to make them shy of coming up to the top tray. Fold some newspaper and place it on top of the food scraps or put on a worm blanket if you think that light is getting in.

Mites

Mites are tiny white or red bugs you may see in your worm bin.

It is critical to know the difference between red mites and white mites:
White mites are not harmful; in fact, they are one of the beneficial decomposing creatures. They can, however, suddenly overpopulate, and then they will be competing with your worms for the food.

Red mites eat worms. You do not want to tolerate them in your bin at all.

Here are a few ways to lessen or get rid of mites in your worm bin:

Mites like an acidic and wet environment. Put a few pieces of watermelon rind or potato peels on the top of the worm bin. This will draw white mites, and you can pull the pieces out and get rid of vast numbers of them.

A damp newspaper page will also attract them, and you can throw it away (I recommend putting them in a plastic bag to ensure they don't travel).[80]

To avoid white mite explosions in the future, be careful of the moisture and acidic content of your food scraps as you add them to your bin[81] Also, make sure you are not overfeeding your worms. If it is a super great environment for mites, it is *not* great for your worms.

Fruit Flies

You know what attracts fruit flies, right? They live up to their name.

Too much fruit will attract them, and all the more so if the worms have not been able to eat it quick enough and it's beginning to rot.

When you add some fruit to your worm bin, try tucking it under some bedding or laying a sheet of newspaper or a worm blanket on top instead of letting the fruit be exposed directly to air.

In some climates, there can be a fruit fly invasion in the summer seasonally. Here are some useful tools:

- A fruit fly trap is an excellent way to protect your worm bin along with covering the top of your food scraps. A bowl of apple cider vinegar and 1 drop of liquid dish soap set next to your bin can help trap them. Be sure to change it every day.[82]
- Flypaper strips
- A mesh screen cut to size to go on top of your bin as well so that the flies can't get through to lay larvae.

Also, best practices in the care of your worm bin will automatically eliminate a lot of the attraction of fruit flies:

- Don't overfeed them
- Make sure the food is not rotten when you put it in
- Cover the food with bedding, newspaper or a worm blanket

Centipedes

Watch for centipedes as they are worm killers. They use their pinchers to poison and paralyze the worms and eat them.

You have to remove these by hand; there are no attractants that fool them. They are attracted to your worms.

Use gloves, while they are not poisonous to humans, their stings will *hurt!*[83]

Potworms

Potworms are not harmful to your worms, but they can overpopulate and compete with your worms for food.

If you want to get a bunch of them out, they will respond in great numbers to bread soaked with milk. You can then lift out the bread and potworms by the dozens.[84]

Worms Want to Escape[85]

Worms will have no reason to want to leave your bin if they are well fed and have the right moisture and air. If your worms want to escape, they are either not fed enough, or are having a *"danger, danger get me out of here!"* response for survival.

Check all the critical elements of your bin:

Moisture and Air
They might be suffocating if it's too wet or too dry.
     If too wet, add bedding or dry leaves, aerate. Rescue the worms and replace the bin layers if it all got overly soaked to be redeemable.
     If too dry, spray some unchlorinated water in the bin (you can get the chlorine out of the water just by leaving some out overnight).

Make sure they have enough food.
When was the last time you checked the bin? Is all of the food gone? Did you leave too long of a time interval between feedings?

Did they have too much food and it's going rotten?
An anaerobic environment will harm and kill them. They would want out.

Is it dark enough?

You can put mesh screen over your aeration holes if needed, but a well-kept worm bin will keep happy worms from wandering.

Worms are dying

They probably tried to escape but couldn't. If they start to die, it will be for all the same reasons that they try to escape:

- Too wet or dry
- Not enough air
- Not enough food
- Too much food
- Too hot or too cold
- A centipede invasion could cause a worm die-off in theory, but I'm not sure that has ever happened. In any case, be observant and make sure there are no centipedes in your bin.

Review the troubleshooting tips and explanations under maintenance to correct these things.

Harvesting Worm Castings

From a plastic tub, cinderblock or any other kind of bin that is not a pyramid

2-3 weeks before you think you'll be ready to harvest your worms, start feeding them on one side of the bin. This will encourage the worms to move over to one side, meaning that you won't have to separate so many from the worm castings you want to harvest on the other side.

Carefully scoop the worm castings out of the bin (there will still be a worm here and there in it, relocate them to the food side). Use a dirt sifter like this to sift out larger chunks and let the castings go into a bin or container of your choice.

https://www.amazon.com/Fox-Peak-Outdoor-Supply-Trapping/dp/B07VZ5L75K/ref=sr_1_41?dchild=1&keywords=sifter&qid=1589671846&sr=8-41

Here is a great video doing this from a plastic tub, but you can imagine how well it will work for any bin. https://www.youtube.com/watch?v=NLJJf0k_v2w

From a Pyramid Bin

The bottom tray has your worm castings; you may need to strain them, or not. There might be some worms in there, but very few as they will be up at the top seeking food.

Storing Worm Castings

Ideally, you would use your worm castings right away instead of storing them. You *want* the microbes which will support your soil. Having said that, if you are in a place with a snowy winter and an indoor worm bin, you might find yourself needing to store for a few months before the snow melts, and you can apply your worm castings to your garden or landscape.

If you do have to store them for a few months (best no longer than six most), then keep the worm castings at 20% moisture level to keep the microbes alive. You can put them in a bag that is breathable, and make sure don't dry out.

If you have a pyramid system, you can let the worm castings stay in the trays (check them for moisture) and add trays on top during the winter months. Make sure you have enough trays for the worm composter that you have to accommodate a break in harvesting the castings and releasing the tray for a new top tray.

Harvesting Your Worms as They Multiply

Worms hate light. They will DIVE down when exposed to light. Both of these methods are based upon "herding" your worms with light.

Harvesting Worms from a Bin Without Trays

If you are using any system other than a pyramid bin with trays, this is the easiest way to harvest your worms:

1) Spread out a tarp in the shade or newspaper inside and arrange to have bright lights over the tarp.
2) Make piles along the tarp in cone shapes.
3) The worms will dive down to get away from the light. Brush off the top layer of the cone, move to the next pile, do the same thing, then come back to the first one you started with.
4) Let the worms move down, repeat moving the top till you see worms then go to the next pile.
5) At the bottom, you will have a bunch of worms who will be much happier in the dark container with air holes that you have prepared for them.

6) Reassemble the layers of your worm bin from the piles on the tarp, making sure that the most finished worm castings are on the bottom and the food is at the top. You can use this opportunity to separate any pieces of food that were not wholly eaten out of the castings in more advanced stages and put them back into the top with your food scraps.

7) You've got a bunch of worms, now what? The best thing is to put the worms directly into your garden. If you are transporting them, put them in a dark container with air. They can be put into a refrigerator which will slow them down. Just make sure they have the right moisture level.

Harvesting Worms with a Pyramid Tray System

The same principle applies if you have a tray system in a pyramid bin; it's just easier.

1) Lay out a newspaper or tarp. You can do this inside if you want.

2) Take an empty tray and put a worm blanket or a couple of layers of newspaper in the bottom so the worms can't migrate down. Place this tray on the tarp or newspaper on the ground or floor.

3) Put the tray you want to use to harvest worms on top of the empty one.

4) Shine a *bright* light onto the top of the tray, continuously. You can use a tactical flashlight or a bright lamp. Gently lift the contents of the tray to expose them to the light as they dive to get away from it.

5) Repeat with trays until you have the number of worms you want to harvest.

6) Ideally, put the harvested worms into your garden or potted plants. If you are transporting them to someone else, put them in a dark container with air holes. They can go into a refrigerator to slow them down and help them sleep.

Now you know how to:
- Choose the right worm bin system for you.
- Get set up with your bin.
- Maintain your worms
- Harvest your worm castings
- Harvest your worms

Vermicomposting might work as your only compost method. You also might use it along with other composting systems like a garden waste pile outside, a tumbler, or even an indoor compost bucket if you have too many food scraps to support a small indoor worm bin.

Part Three:
Humanure Composting

Introduction
o **Historical Context**
o **FAQ**

Chapter One: **Set up a Compost Toilet**
　　　　　　　　o Build a Compost Toilet Bucket System
　　　　　　　　o Ready-made Compost Toilets

Chapter Two: Use & Maintain Your Compost Toilet

　　　　　　　　o Prep your compost Toilet for Use
　　　　　　　　o Use & Maintenance

Chapter Three: Setup & Maintain Your Humanure Compost Pile

　　　　　　　　o **Prep your Humanure Compost Pile**
　　　　　　　　o **Killing Pathogens with Temperatures & Time**

Conclusion

Introduction

For most environmentally conscious people, actions like composting or having worm composting are relatively easy to step into once the issues of smell and mess are addressed. If you mention humanure, it's a different story. There may be outright rejection or a longer arch of learning and acceptance.

Scepticism or rejection is understandable. Both rotting food and waste trigger a primal response in our bodies to pull back and get away – for good reason! Pathogens and micro-organisms that will make us very sick or be life-threatening are in there, and our bodies know it. [86]

There are areas in the world where cesspools leach into agriculture or wells. Also sometimes flooding causes raw sewage to pour into crops or water supplies. Both situations are known for cholera outbreaks. It's not that unusual to see Norovirus outbreaks in urban areas simply from people not washing their hands after going to the bathroom. Modern people regularly get conjunctivitis that way as well. Harmful parasitic worms are also a risk from exposure to raw sewage.

You can relax, I'm not going to tell you that your sense of caution and disgust is unwarranted or that you are supposed to tolerate either smell or pathogens.

Humanure is not raw sewage.
Humanure does not smell.
It is as safe as any other compost to put on your vegetables.

Making humanure does not have to be difficult or gross.

92

There is more to the story of that "Ew! Get away!" response, than just our natural protective instincts. There is powerful conditioning in the modern culture about our urine and poop. We are conditioned to believe that any way of dealing with our poop other than flushing it away so it "disappears" (to us) is dirty, gross and unsafe.

Composting our poop into humanure is none of those things.

It's interesting how we are entirely adapted to spreading cow and horse manure over gardens, but so many of us tend to have such a strong gross-out or fear response to humanure.

Also, there are commercial products that are labelled as "compost" that include biosolids from sewers. These solids have been heated to kill the pathogens as well as the beneficial micro-organisms. [87]

So, while holding all due respect towards safety concerns and the gag factor of poop smell, let's get some context and apply some rationality. Then we can discern whether humanure might be a great idea.

A Brief Historical Context

For as long as we've been around as a species hunting and gathering,
humans have been working with the earth to compost our urine and waste.

Tribes figured out how to manage large clusters of people in one place by having "latrines" which were large deep holes or trenches dug with soil or other material nearby to add on top of each deposit. When it was about 2/3 full, it was ready to close. The square of the earth that was removed to dig the hole was replaced on top. The microbes and plants then processed the waste. The latrine system is still the most common method for large hunting camps and other backcountry events with more than four people.

Fast forward to human settlements through millennia: Attica, Hong Kong, China, Singapore, Japan, Mexico, Central America, India, the US and the UK are among those to have used sewage for fertilizer. [88] Clearly, this is not an exhaustive list and includes recent history. In Japan and India, there are present-day practices.

What happened in large cities in the late 1800s and early 20th century explains, I believe, some of why our cultural conditioning is so intense around humanure.

Before the installation of sewage systems in New York, farms purchased "night soil" (raw human waste) from cesspools and privies. Night soil is not composted in any way. On the east coast, the night soil was collected in New York and transferred to the farmland in Long Island and Staten Island. [89]

> "Night soil" was removed from privies under the cloak of darkness so that polite society would be spared from confronting its own feces as the men carted the crap away, leaving a trail of stench in their wake. Each year in cities across the country, thousands of carts brimming with excrement rattled through the night streets. This was an antiquated solution to a modern problem: America's cities were full of crap.
>
> As cities grew larger and denser in the 19th century, the paltry urban infrastructure could not handle the sheer tonnage of human waste its residents were producing. New York was the dirtiest city of them all. In 1844 it was estimated that Manhattanites alone produced nearly 800,000 cubic feet of excrement – that's enough poop to fill the trunks of about 53,000 mid-sized cars.
>
> In addition to the assault on human senses, this system had disastrous public health consequences. Leaky cesspools and overflowing privies created fetid pools of standing water that leached into the soil and contaminated local water wells. This

94

*fueled cholera epidemics well into the nineteenth century, such
as the 1849 outbreak, which claimed 5,000 lives in New York
City alone.* [90]

Can you imagine living in New York or one of the other cities at
the time? If someone came to you and suggested that a flush sewer
system could make this go away, what do you think would be your
response? My response would be: *"Take my money!"*

We have to realize that if you live in the US, the people described
in that quote are our ancestors and formed a large part of our
cultural heritage. Other countries had their equivalent journey in
the 19th and early 20th centuries as they dealt with the challenge of
growing human density in cities and human waste.   It was not too
long ago that our ancestors experienced both this ordeal *and* the
solution of sewers that drastically changed their quality of life.

With that history, *of course*, we have been culturally conditioned
to be so attached to our sewer systems! Sewers solved a lot of
horrific problems. Or so it seemed.

Sadly, when we designed and installed those sewer systems, we
had lost the ancient human wisdom of composting but not yet
gained the modern scientific knowledge to design systems that
could quickly turn "night soil" into safe humanure. There was a
sense that the earth was a "resource" for us, and the oceans and
waterways had an infinite capacity for any waste we poured in.
That philosophy has caught up to us: Now we are waking up to the
fact that it was misguided: much to the detriment of the earth,
including our own species.   The appalling problems that were
solved by sewer systems were replaced by other horrific problems
that were slower to be visible.

Now we face the challenges of the 21st century. The earth's
systems are buckling under the weight of humanity's ways of
living, including waste disposal. We have also made massive
progress in scientific technology and understanding. We can learn

to apply techniques and practices such as humanure safely and beneficially.

Humanure is *not* night soil. It is our composted waste turned to humus that does not smell and has beneficial micro-organisms ready to assist any vegetable garden or landscaping.

Now that we've established the facts let's look at the next question: "Why should I bother?"

I am composting and worm composting, why should I bother with humanure?

Environmental Reasons for Humanure

Water conservation:
In homes with flush toilets, an average individual uses 6600 gallons of water a year for flushing.[91]
Multiply by 326 million people in the US = 2,151,600,000,000
Leaving out the 151.5 *billion* gallons to accommodate infants and the widespread adoption of low flush toilets:

That is **over two trillion** *gallons of drinkable water a year in the US used for* **flushing alone**

In conventional systems, the water in your toilet is the same as the water coming out of your kitchen tap. We are not using rainwater or greywater for this purpose, so the waste is even more poignant.

Water Contamination:

That two trillion gallons (in the US alone) of what was potable water is filled with excrement and goes into streams, rivers, lakes, waterways and the oceans. All of these bodies of water are impacted by the raw or partially treated sewage that is pumped into them, making them undrinkable and dangerous.

<u>Our poop needs to go somewhere, if not the waterways, then where?</u>

As of January 2020, there are 7.8 billion people on earth. Approximately 329,500,000 of them in the US. Many of us are densely populated in relatively small geographic areas, and all of us are pooping every day. We need to do *something* with our human waste.

This article is not about the possibilities for large scale humanure use, but the same principles apply to individuals and households who want to save water and reduce waste. Since humanure is excellent for the soil, we can turn our poop into an untapped resource, save a lot of water and avoid a lot of pollution.

<u>Practical Reasons for Humanure:</u>

You may be considering a compost toilet for practical reasons such as:

- You may have an outbuilding or tiny house that does not have easy access to a toilet and no water connection. Installing plumbing is a considerable cost.
- You may have a primary residence without running water access.
- You may have outer areas of land where toilet access is not convenient.
- You may want more high-quality compost!

FAQs

Why Not Just Use a Chemical Port-A-Potty?

Short Answer: Chemical toilets smell *terrible* and include chemicals that are harmful to the environment.

If you are concerned about the smell, a chemical toilet is not the answer. Have you ever used one? It smells like poop with chemical fragrance overlaid on top of it. That's precisely what it is. Those fragrances don't do a good job of hiding anything; they just smell sickly and weird on top of poop.

Yuck.

A compost toilet doesn't smell!

Older versions of chemical toilets had formaldehyde in them. This was dangerous to humans: 1) could cause skin irritation or blisters if water splashed up on your buttocks, 2) it is very harmful to breathe 3) 1&2 put workers at risk and 3) it kills aquatic wildlife.

Fortunately, we have moved away from formaldehyde in modern chemical toilets. When you rent a port-a-potty, it will be using micro-organisms and enzymes to breakdown the waste. Even so, it will still include toxic chemicals and fragrances.

Even though the added use of micro-organisms and enzymes is *better* than *only* using harmful chemicals, the toilet needs to be changed every seven days before the microbes and enzymes die. [92] (Also, they still include chemicals that will be dumped into the sewer systems and eventually waterways.)

Long term chemical toilets rarely get changed every seven days, so after a week the smell gets worse and worse until it's full. Do your cost analysis of having a port-a-potty that is emptied every week. After you've set up a compost toilet, the cost is zero to sawdust.

I would much prefer to use a compost toilet than a chemical toilet, any day.

What is that "poop smell"?

Short Answer: Bacteria farting.

When we poop, along with the discarded matter of our food, comes bacteria from our gut. We have literally trillions of them inside us, and some of them get swept up and pooped out in the process of digestion and excretion.

These bacteria give off-gas. Most gut bacteria release odorless hydrogen, carbon dioxide and methane. The bacterial gasses that smell are sulfur-based. [93] These are the bacteria that make our poop smell.

Do compost toilets have a lot of flies?

Short Answer: No. It's straightforward to keep the flies down. If you do have a problem in the peak summer season, it's easy to troubleshoot.

Add sawdust to cover every deposit, keep the seat lid closed.

If you live in an area where there tend to be dramatic spikes in the number of flies during the summer, you may consider making sure you empty your bucket every 12-13 days. (The eggs incubate for two weeks.)

You may be using a system where you don't empty the bucket but just seal it when it's full. If this is the case, then a practical and effective solution is to spray diluted neem oil (your garden center or hardware store will have this), around the sides and in the bucket. Typically, a few days will be an effective deterrent, and it will also kill eggs.[94]

Can I have a compost toilet outside in cold winters?

Short answer: Yes!

When it gets very cold or freezes, the composting just slows down or stops. It can pick back up again.

One humanure composter from Alaska posted on a forum that they were super happy with the way that humanure composting was working, even in their wintry

Environment. Temperatures were below freezing for three weeks (-24F) and the humanure compost pile they had outside was still 112F! [95]

How often will I have to empty or change over my compost toilet?

for two people in full-time use, a 5-gallon bucket will be filled 3/4 full in about 3-4 days
-for two people in full-time use, one 55-gallon barrel will be filled in about two months
-for two people in full-time use, about 0.5 to 1 gallon of urine per day will accumulate in the urine bucket.
http://www.omick.net/composting_toilets/bucket_barrel_to
ilet.htm

Can I pee in my compost toilet?

Short answer: Yes, but there are downsides to using your poop bucket to pee in exclusively.

Going back to basic composting principles that we have discussed earlier:
- There is carbon to nitrogen ratio at work for composting.
- Moisture content is also a factor for effective composting.

If you pee in your poop bucket as you pee in a flush toilet, you will end up with

- A lot of nitrogen
- A lot of liquid

Poop buckets don't have holes in the bottom for obvious reasons; they are totally sealed. Therefore, if you do decide to use your compost toilet for peeing in the same way as a flush toilet, then you will have to have a lot more carbon (e.g. sawdust) to absorb it. This will mean that you will have to empty or change over your bucket much more often (at least twice as much, maybe more).

The liquid and nitrogen are why most humanure composters choose to either pee outdoors or make a pee bucket for those times when that's all you need.

Separate pee bucket:

Pee buckets are emptied every day and mixed with three parts of water to one-part urine and added to the soil of plants. You can add it straight to vegetables and fruits. It does not contain pathogens and is high in nitrogen, potassium and phosphorus (10:1:4).

- Cautions for emptying diluted pee buckets directly on plants:
   1) Along with the great nutrients, urine is also loaded with salt; so don't add it consistently to the same plants.
   2) Urine is twice as high in nitrogen as your average plant food, so you can easily burn your plants by adding it without dilution.

No pee bucket:

If you choose not to have a separate pee bucket, you have two options:

1) Peeing in your poop bucket and changing it a lot more often because of the extra liquid and nitrogen content.
2) Pee outside

Peeing outside is a widespread practice for humanure composters who have ample outdoor space and privacy. Just rotate around, don't pee in the same place a lot. Some people put a pee bucket on their porch when it's raining hard.

If you want a compost toilet for an outbuilding or remote part of your land where it's a long way back to the bathroom, then you probably don't have a hose for water there either. Therefore, diluting the pee in a bucket would be a challenge. If this is the case, you might consider peeing outside. At the very least, when you empty the bucket, you need to sprinkle it around so that not too much is going on place or the plants will turn brown and possibly die.

Urine diverting kit:

I see these as getting the best of both worlds. I don't want to have an extra pee bucket in my compost toilet room, but I also don't want to have the extra work of accommodating all that urine in my poop bucket.

Enter, the urine-diverting kit. You **do** have an extra pee bucket, but it is next to the poop bucket, and the tube diverts it over. You still need to empty it every day, but you don't have to have two seats.

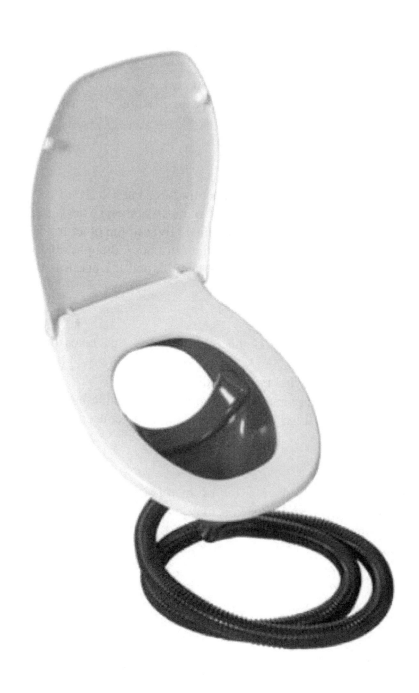

https://www.shoptinyhouses.com/products/separett-privy-501-urine-diverting-toilet-kit?variant=27702614281
https://morningchores.com/diy-composting-toilet/
Here is another option with some great reviews: https://www.etsy.com/listing/778670899/diy-compost-toilet-urine-diverter-and?ref=search_srv-1&frs=1

I've only used one of these once before, but I have to tell you I loved it. I didn't have to worry about whether I was just peeing going to poop as well, and then move over to the other toilet seat if I thought I was just peeing and then my body thought otherwise. I just sat down, all happened as it should, and the pee was diverted to a separate bucket!

In short,
- Peeing outside is the easiest option that takes the least space.
- Second to that is a urine diverter.
- Many humanure composters do use double buckets though, it isn't that difficult, and you get used to it.

Summary

Now we've looked at a bit of history and context for compost toilets, and why you may want to include one in your life. When asked "Why should I want to set up a compost toilet?", I think this blog said it perfectly:

> *"No water, no drains, no smell, no hassle, and a regular supply of inert, safe, soil-smelling compost (humanure) to add to your garden compost heap."*[96]

Let's turn our attention to choosing a compost toilet, how to build one and maintain it to turn your waste into humanure.

Chapter One: How to Set up a Compost Toilet

There are many options for setting up compost toilets; you can purchase stand-alone compost toilets, or you can build them inside or out.

For this book, we are talking about using a compost toilet as:

- An addition to a flush toilet;
    or
- for a tiny house or another outbuilding;
    or
- for a place on your land that does not have convenient access to your indoor toilet;
    or
- you may live in a place without plumbing and can set up compost toilets exclusively.

This article will give you simple guidelines and DIY information to apply to your indoor bathroom or make a compost toilet outside. However, it does not address major home renovation of removing a current flush toilet and redesigning an entire indoor bathroom.

You are responsible for checking for any codes, laws, permits, etc. in your location regarding compost toilets.

How to Build a Compost Toilet

We are going to start with the basic need: A stable place to sit, and a bucket.

- This will apply to any compost toilet, indoor or out.

From there, we can look at options for privacy, some of which include building the support as you build the whole structure.

Building the Toilet Bucket Support

<u>A wood cabinet</u>:

Building a wood cabinet as a base and surround for your compost buckets is the most common approach to a basic compost toilet system.

Below are photos of a basic, solid surround for one bucket. Simply put, you want a 24"X24" box with a hinged lid that has a hole in it. You then install a toilet seat on top.

You can make a two-bucket system to include a pee bucket by making the box 24"X48". This design can apply anywhere, inside or out.

In the photos below, the urine bucket is on the left of the first photo. I personally think this makes too much "room for error" in the form of urine spills (yuck). I strongly recommend just making a cabinet surround that accommodates two buckets and either having two comfy seats or using the urine diverter.

I've used some compost toilets that had extended surrounds to make space on the outside of the seat(s) or in the middle to keep toilet paper, hand sanitizer and an open box for personal items like a phone. You can even build space to accommodate reading material!

Think about the size you want for your surround and any extra "creature comforts" that you would like to design. Below are photos of the basic idea:

http://www.omick.net/composting_toilets/bucket_barrel_toilet.htm

Note the second photo where you can see the hole in the lid. It is made so that there is a snug fit around the bucket. This helps keep flies down.

Since many people will want to build a double seat compost toilet for peeing and pooping, here is a video for the double seat option. [97]h ttps://www.youtube.com/watch?v=Jkk5pMJSv5E

108

This is a very detailed tutorial in making a two-bucket compost toilet cabinet. He is using the space for the second bucket for the sawdust; I would use it for the pee bucket. He takes two hours to make it, and he'll be with you every step of the way with explanations of the tools and measurements he is using.
https://www.youtube.com/watch?v=dPdnMuokEw8

Note that if you use a urine diverter, you don't need to have a hole and toilet seat in the top, just a place for the pee bucket in the cabinet.

If your compost toilet is outdoors, another feature you can think about is building the cabinet without a back, so it is against the wall of the structure. The structure is then made with a *hinged back door* so that you can access the bucket(s) from the outside to change them over for new ones. This is a real plus if you are the compost toilet tender.

Remember that you will need space for a bucket of sawdust, wood shavings or peat moss next to the compost toilet.

Medical Toilet Base:

This is super easy. You can get two of them and set them side by side for pee and poop, or you could use the urine diverter above and have the pee bucket next to the medical toilet base.

Obviously, if you choose this system, you will need some other shelving or table for toilet paper, hand sanitizer and personal items.

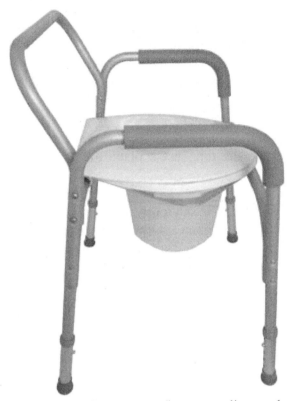

https://www.motherearthnews.com/homesteading-and-livestock/self-reliance/compost-toilet-ze0z1209zhar

Building an Outdoor Compost Toilet Shed as a "Privy"

Tip: Don't try searching for ways to build a "privy" because 1) you'll get a bunch of instructions about making a cesspool (that's basically what privies were) and 2) they will all only have one bucket. This is OK if you are committed to peeing outside, but I have curated a couple of sound instructions for modern compost toilet shelters.

Here you can download a free .pdf for an outhouse building. I make two strong recommendations if you use this plan:

1) It has room for two buckets – adjust the placement of the toilet seat(s) for either two seats or to have the pee bucket underneath the shelf with a urine diverter. The urine diverter option saves space because you can use the extra shelf space for your sawdust bucket.
2) Make a hinged door(s) at the back to empty the bucket.

These people offer a number of examples for a variety of compost toilets and the shelters for them. https://www.5dog.farm/random/compost-toilet-construction/

A well explained tour of a compost toilet building
https://www.youtube.com/watch?v=FJRquNT6Sk0

This woman is clear and concise. You can clearly see the back of the building with the hinged door for bucket changing access as well as additional features like a light, a shelf and a toilet paper holder.

Mennonite Compost Toilet shelter
https://www.youtube.com/watch?v=Qx_qL6YYK9E

Fast forward to 1:27 to get past the intro and see the building.

4:03, he shows you an example of the hinged door at the back of the building that enables the compost tenders to empty and replace the buckets easily from the back of the building.

This is clearly a well-made, sturdy building. If you have building experience, you will be able to figure out how to replicate this. If you love this building, check with the nearest Mennonite community to your location to see if they might be able to build one for you.

Tip for setting up: When you start a new bucket, if you have some straw to put in the bottom (about 5") then put in the wood chip or sawdust or peat moss to about ½ full. Make a hole in the center before you use it. This way it will help.

OK, you've set up your compost toilet, now how do I maintain it, so all goes well?

Ready-Made Compost Toilets

Here are two self-contained compost toilets. I have only included these two because so many other options are either very tiny (intended for RV or camping use only) or not really composting toilets. Watch out for others which require plastic bags, include water flushing and recommend dumping the waste into a sewage system or landfill. Both of these toilets below are compatible with true composting into humanure.

Nature's Head Compost Toilet $925-$950

The number one compost toilet that has great reviews for the product, quality and customer service is the Nature's Head Compost Toilet. Here is their site where you can find FAQ and a detailed user guide. https://natureshead.net/user_guide/ One of the best things about this toilet is that two people using it full time will only have to empty it once every three weeks.

Laveo Dry Flush Composting Toilet $684

This toilet comes with a battery to enable a "flush" function. https://www.shoptinyhouses.com/collections/composting-toilet/products/laveo-dry-flush-toilet

The problem I have with these is that I would spend roughly $700-$1000 and **still** have to empty the bucket! If you are putting your compost toilet in a guest house or other place where you want something that looks nice, you can build (or have built) a beautiful wood cabinet with a toilet seat for your bucket. I've never used a purchased compost toilet before (except in an RV), and they look like *more* work than a bucket system – especially if you use a urine diverter. Then again, some people want something that *looks* like a flush toilet to feel comfortable using it, so you have options.

Chapter Two:
Use and Maintain your Compost Toilet[98]

Prep Your Compost Toilet for Use

After you have acquired your chosen compost toilet system, you need to set it up and get it ready for use.

If you have purchased a compost toilet, follow the user guide for setup. If you are using a bucket system, fill the bucket about ½ full with sawdust.

Experienced user tip: Make a hole in the center of the sawdust (but leave about 5" of sawdust at the bottom). This will help keep the poop from making a cone-shaped pile on top.

<u>A word about sawdust or other carbon-rich material</u>:

You will need to have a bucket of dry carbon-rich material with a scoop next to your compost toilet for use with every deposit. This can be a mix of materials like wood ash, sawdust, fine wood chip, dried leaves, a little straw or peat moss. It can also be just one fine-textured thing. It is not recommended to use straw exclusively for this purpose as it doesn't help the decomposition of the poop as fast as finer materials. Also, wood ash is OK mixed in, but not as the only thing because of the dust and lack of the hungry decomposing enzymes that the other materials have.

Make sure that your sawdust or wood chip is not from treated or painted wood. It's going into compost, and chemical treatments (some of which are petroleum/plastic-based) don't break down.

Also, if you are using sawdust or wood chip, try to get *fresh* material from a local woodworker or building site. Do some research; sometimes they will happily give away fresh sawdust that you can load up by the pickup or trailer full. If you can't find fresh, you can purchase bags of sawdust from DIY centers, but it will lack the sugars and lively enzymes that tackle the decomposition super quickly. Fresh sawdust, for example, has sugars in it that eat up the bacteria and make the poop smell vanish. You open the toilet lid, and it smells like wood, it's amazing.

Using Your Compost Toilet

Place a bucket of sawdust, fine wood shavings or peat moss with a scoop in it next to your compost toilet. After each deposit, *cover it completely* with the sawdust (or equivalent). You don't want to bury it deeply but cover it (about 1") to prevent odor and flies. Then close the toilet seat lid.

Toilet paper is fine to put in your compost toilet, it decomposes.

Maintenance of Your Compost Toilet

Empty the poop bucket:

Once your bucket is ½-3/4 full, take it to your humanure compost pile, empty it and cover it with another layer of dry carbon-rich material.

But, wait! Will it be really smelly and gross to empty out the poop bucket?

Short Answer: Not really.

Remember, the reason poop smells the way it does is because of the bacteria that releases sulfurous gasses. The poop already began to decompose in the bucket while it was being filled. By the time you empty it, almost all of the smell has gone.

Rinse out the bucket:

Plastic is a porous material. Metal buckets are too heavy for maintenance for most people. We keep a sturdy toilet brush and a bin full of baking soda next to the humanure compost pile.

- Empty out the bucket, cover the deposit,
- then rinse out the emptied bucket into the compost pile (never the ground),
- then put a handful of baking soda into the bucket and give it a scrub with the toilet brush,
- rinse again, emptying the water onto the compost pile.

Empty the pee bucket:

Don't wait till it's full! Empty the pee bucket at about ½-2/3 full otherwise it's hard to handle.

You can fill it with water and put it into your food scrap compost pile (urine does not contain pathogens like poop) or dilute it to 1-part urine to 4-parts water and put it directly onto the soil of your garden or landscaping.

Chapter Three:
Maintain the Humanure Compost Pile

Prep your Humanure Compost Pile

If you haven't already, you'll need to set up your designated humanure compost pile. Obviously, *this must be done before you empty your first bucket!*

The pallet bin system that was described in the compost section is recommended for humanure. Lay down a layer (about 5") of straw/sawdust/dried leaves, woodchip or other dry material on the bottom. Wood ash can also be included, but not a good choice to use exclusively as this base layer.

It is also recommended to have either a pallet bin section or another container ready with dry material such as dried leaves or straw. This way, when you empty your bucket, your materials will be ready.

Killing Pathogens with Temperature and Time

It is useful to understand the temperatures and time required to ensure that the harmful pathogens are killed in your humanure pile. Unless you are doing cold composting of your humanure pile, I highly recommend a compost thermometer. They are very useful for any hot or warm composting system, and in the case of humanure, ensure safety, confidence and peace of mind. Make sure you have one like this with a 20" stem. https://www.amazon.com/REOTEMP-Backyard-Compost-Thermometer-

Instructions/dp/B002P5RGMI/ref=sr_1_3?dchild=1&keywords=c
ompost+thermometer&qid=1590524210&sr=8-3
Temperatures and Time It Takes To Kill Pathogens:[99]

Here is a list of times it takes to destroy the dangerous pathogens:

109.4F   1 month
114.8F   1 week
122F   1 day
143.6F   1 hour
149F   A few minutes

You can see that having a compost thermometer is key if you want to harvest humanure as quickly as possible. Also, note that just because the pathogens are killed does not mean that the humanure is finished compost.

Unattended Cold and Warm Humanure Composting:

You may not be attached to how quickly you can use your humanure, and you may not want to have to watch the temperature of your humanure compost pile. If that is the case, then you can just let it go for two years and harvest it after that. I have a friend who harvested layers of humanure from his pallet bin pile that was two years old. It came out as rich and beautiful humus, ready for his garden.

Do I have to turn and aerate my humanure compost?

Short and only answer: No. Don't. Not if you are using a humanure compost pile. Just let it be, keeping the carbon material balance right when you empty a bucket.

Humanure Conclusion

Like it or not, humans make a lot of waste. Our modern western way of dealing with it has lulled us into a feeling that it just disappears, and all is fine. Now we know better. With drought, water pollution and the need to enrich our topsoil, the sewer system has become a "ball and chain" rather than the clean, elegant solution it seemed to be when it was introduced to our cities.

With some attention to set up and a little bit of maintenance, a humanure compost system can save a lot of water and give you a rich soil amendment for your garden.

Our waste has to go somewhere, why not cycle it back, enrich our gardens and keep it out of our waterways?

Conclusion

Composting has so many benefits. To start with, we get free fertilizer for our gardens and landscaping that cycles back our own waste! Free fertilizer and plant food are ours with just a bit of planning and attention.

There are, however, bigger and more weightier reasons that composting is worth our time and effort.

We live in a time when the 3.8-billion-year-old life systems of the earth are beginning to collapse. In the Arctic and Antarctic regions, there are ice sheets and glaciers that have been key to the temperature regulation of the entire planet. They are melting at alarming rates; sea levels are rising. Unpredictable natural disasters and extreme temperatures all tell us that climate change is upon us.

California experienced a severe 7-year drought. By the end of it, the photos of the reservoirs at their lowest points were alarming and frightening; One could not help but wonder "What happens if this doesn't end?" I often ask myself "What *would* have happened if it had not ended?" Water scarcity is of great concern amongst scientists and governments globally. Some have even said "water is the new oil". [100]

As news cycles unfold every day, it is common for us mere mortal citizens to feel completely overwhelmed in the face of massive threats and grim statistics.

Composting our food scraps, garden waste and even our feces can be a way that we exert power over our personal and collective environmental impact. We can significantly lower our CO_2 emissions and landfill impact by simply composting. Each one of us can save approximately 6600 gallons of water a year if we compost our poop.

We now step into the challenges of our lifetime. Together we have power to alter the effects of humanity's over-consumption. Our waste has to go somewhere, let's do our best to manage it so the next generations do not bear the heavy cost of our denial.

Appendix 1:
The Essential Science of Compost

There are three areas of essential science that helps any composter understand the compost process. You don't have to have a science degree to understand some valuable basics.

1) Aerobic and Anaerobic Bacteria
2) The C:N (Carbon to Nitrogen) Ratio
3) The Three Phases of Composting

1) Aerobic and Anaerobic Bacteria[101]

All bacteria are single cell microbes. Microbes are any tiny living organisms, they may or may not be bacteria.

We are looking at two kinds of bacteria: aerobic and anaerobic.

Aerobic bacteria must have oxygen. They use nitrogen, phosphorus, potassium and other nutrients in the compost to live and do not give off horrible smelling gasses.

Anaerobic bacteria cannot tolerate oxygen. They are missing enzymes that are required to tolerate it. Oxygen is actually toxic to anaerobic bacteria which is the scientific reason why "fresh air" is a common cure for unpleasant household smells. Anaerobic bacteria die when exposed to oxygen.

Anaerobic decomposition (also called putrefaction) works more slowly than aerobic decomposition. It also emits mostly methane but also other gasses such as and hydrogen sulfide that are identified as "rotting" or "putrid", "rotting eggs" or "something dead" (all accurate).

The C:N (Carbon to Nitrogen) Ratio
As we've discussed, your browns are your carbon-rich sources for your compost, and the greens are the nitrogen-rich. The ratio is approximately 2-parts browns to 1-part greens.

Knowing this, you might find it confusing to read scientific information talking about the carbon to nitrogen (C:N) ratio being 25-30:1.

Wait, what?

Why is there such a huge discrepancy in this information?

This is not conflicting information. When the scientific articles are talking about a 25-30:1 ratio, they are referencing the chemical/molecular structure which is (clearly) vastly different than the ratio of the *amounts of material.*

The C:N ratio of 25-30:1 does NOT translate
to putting 30 parts of browns to 1 part of greens!

The C:N ratio translates to 2-parts of browns to 1-part
greens.

The Three Phases of Composting

These three stages are temperature based. It is the process of the compost heating up and cooling down. Each phase, of course provides different functions. For professional farmers or those selling compost, there can be a fourth stage, "curing". For our purposes here's a summary of three:

123

The primary or *mesophilic* stage which lasts for a couple of days to a couple of weeks (depending on the size of your compost and weather if applicable).

The secondary or *thermophilic* stage is the hottest temperature and is the most active stage of decomposition with the greatest number of microbes.

The finishing "cooling" phase that allows the temperature to cool and the fungi can move in to "finish" your compost.

References

[1] Benefits of Compost?
https://learn.eartheasy.com/guides/composting/
https://www.realmomnutrition.com/how-to-compost-at-home/

2 https://www.epa.gov/recycle/composting-home

https://www.motherearthnews.com/organic-gardening/home-composting-zmaz06onzraw

[3] This is a good explanation of off gassing in landfill: https://www.goingzerowaste.com/blog/composting-for-apartments

https://learn.eartheasy.com/guides/composting/

4
https://www.goodhousekeeping.com/home/gardening/advice/a23945/start-composting/
https://www.budgetdumpster.com/blog/how-to-compost-at-home/

5
https://extension.uga.edu/publications/detail.html?number=B1189&title=Food%20Waste%20Composting:%20Institutional%20and%20Industrial%20Application

https://earth911.com/business-policy/how-commercial-composting-works/
https://www.biocycle.net/2019/01/04/food-waste-composting-infrastructure-u-s/
https://www.urthpact.com/industrial-composting-what-it-is-and-how-it-works/

6 https://sosfuture.org/blogs/news/how-to-compost-at-home?gclid=CjwKCAjwnIr1BRAWEiwA6GpwNblR7u-BcBdmsinRFPc3Bq-rOQUh7Xi7bPSAoX5zmO6eQjg_FiNIvhoCriMQAvD_BwE

7 https://www.motherearthnews.com/organic-gardening/home-composting-zmaz06onzraw

8 Here's an example of a compost thermometer: https://www.grainger.com/product/3JPN4?gclid=Cj0KCQjwhZr1BRCLARIsALjRVQNoyPUgEdYql_wNWG0lP2V9D9ELqv8UOYDGtm3nVIPqVspKMM-kynsaAhazEALw_wcB&cm_mmc=PPC:+Google+PLA&ef_id=Cj0KCQjwhZr1BRCLARIsALjRVQNoyPUgEdYql_wNWG0lP2V9D9ELqv8UOYDGtm3nVIPqVspKMM-kynsaAhazEALw_wcB:G:s&s_kwcid=AL!2966!3!281733071186!!!g!477018736688!

9 Store-Bought vs. Homemade Compost: https://www.google.com/search?q=store+bought+compost&oq=store+bought+compost&aqs=chrome..69i57.4690j0j7&sourceid=chrome&ie=UTF-8

https://squarefoot.forumotion.com/t16666-ingredients-in-store-bought-compost

https://www.gardensalive.com/product/compost-can-you-buy-it-in-a-bag

https://www.houzz.com/discussions/1642914/store-bought-compost

10 https://thrivingyard.com/homemade-vs-bagged-compost/

11 https://www.houzz.com/discussions/1642914/store-bought-compost

[12] https://www.planetnatural.com/best-compost/

[14] https://www.gardensalive.com/product/compost-can-you-buy-it-in-a-bag

[15] https://www.gardensalive.com/product/gardeners-gold-premium-compost

16
https://www.gardeningknowhow.com/composting/ingredients/composting-ashes.htm

17 https://homeguides.sfgate.com/composting-avocado-skins-rinds-38662.html

18 https://www.planetnatural.com/composting-paper/

19 https://learn.eartheasy.com/guides/composting/

20 As a beginner, start with this rule. There is conflicting information about whether these are ok. Also, beware of outdated information. For example, there have been pathogens and diseases in cow manure that has taken it off the list as a safe composting item.

This is more advanced work. The reader is encouraged to do research and get the latest data and information before including manure in compost.

21
https://www.google.com/aclk?sa=L&ai=DChcSEwi4teWckpPpAhUM28AKHcKXCNIYABABGgJpbQ&sig=AOD64_3tKowiiKlAXBeJmyLnfVasF1KePw&q=&ved=2ahUKEwjk19yckpPpAhUQCs0KHaZVApIQ0Qx6BAgOEAE&adurl=

[22] Composting non-organic food scraps - source of info for this section is this article and the scientific agricultural reports listed: https://www.planetnatural.com/composting-101/compost-concerns/pesticides/

23 https://www.bhg.com/gardening/yard/compost/how-to-compost/
https://www.motherearthnews.com/organic-gardening/home-composting-zmaz06onzraw

24 https://www.gardeningchannel.com/hot-cold-warm-composting/

25 https://learn.eartheasy.com/articles/how-to-compost-in-an-apartment/

https://www.apartmenttherapy.com/how-to-make-your-own-indoor-compost-bin-138645

26 Basic plastic countertop compost bin $13
https://www.officesupplysource.com/product/610347/busch-systems-kitchen-composter-solid-lid-2-25g-green/?origin=google_product_ads&gclid=Cj0KCQjwy6T1BRDX ARIsAIqCTXpA--lPH-huYQ1yOXGg079FPLeQGb9hL7ezPDWty8229Os1RqIJeKcaAuj -EALw_wcB

Very stylish stainless steel with a charcoal filter $30
https://www.amazon.com/Utopia-Kitchen-Stainless-Compost-Countertop/dp/B015DRQ36E

27

Bio Bags: https://www.biobagusa.com/
28 https://www.younghouselove.com/younghouselovedotcompost/

https://www.amazon.com/Behrens-Trash-Burner-Composter-Gallon/dp/B000AS78EI/ref=zg_bs_3753631_39?_encoding=UTF 8&psc=1&refRID=NKTZRWVVV3K4EY3T3MCT

[29] Dog Food Bin as Compost Bucket:
https://www.amazon.com/Vittles-Vault-Airtight-Container-Storage/dp/B0002DJOMA/ref=sr_1_52?crid=35IYMSO24E8GO &dchild=1&keywords=dog+food+bins+15+lbs&qid=1588086595 &sprefix=dog+food+bins%2Caps%2C402&sr=8-52

30 This person puts a bucket under their sink
https://www.apartmenttherapy.com/how-to-make-your-own-indoor-compost-bin-138645

31 The Food Cycler
https://www.amazon.com/product-reviews/B06XPQWVLJ/ref=cm_cr_arp_d_viewopt_kywd?ie=UT F8&filterByStar=one_star&reviewerType=all_reviews&pageNum ber=1&filterByKeyword=+disappointed#reviews-filter-bar

32

 https://www.gardeners.com/buy/evolution-pyramid-composter/8600227.html?utm_campaign=PLA&utm_medium=go ogleshopping&utm_source=google&SC=XNET0146&gclid=Cjw KCAjw4pT1BRBUEiwAm5QuRyf7QlGotlFYx8gVHDKU2e5CA YvHccGmQ_hQfGmw3hTZk9wUXMzqzRoCLsQQAvD_BwE

https://www.thekitchn.com/tips-for-setting-up-a-simple-backyard-compost-system-202160

https://www.googleadservices.com/pagead/aclk?sa=L&ai=DChcS EwigxKi-xIHpAhUB28AKHbE-BA8YABAXGgJpbQ&ohost=www.google.com&cid=CAESQOD 2v6I_qoUOXUi801SdR3oL2ITUm1QSJTKpNrKRoADAGXIW0 XX_dxFUmHSC3pBQ6e-

JgF08XcRzQHxmrymBw9Q&sig=AOD64_25aIvF_3yTDK2JQdy
3szFJrDzMuA&ctype=5&q=&ved=2ahUKEwiu2Z2-
xIHpAhWQVs0KHXKUBUYQ9aACegQIDRBZ&adurl=

[33] https://www.amazon.com/Behrens-Trash-Burner-Composter-Gallon/dp/B000AS78EI/ref=zg_bs_3753631_39?_encoding=UTF
8&psc=1&refRID=NKTZRWVVV3K4EY3T3MCT

34 https://www.younghouselove.com/younghouselovedotcompost/

35 https://www.amazon.com/Behrens-Trash-Burner-Composter-Gallon/dp/B000AS78EI/ref=zg_bs_3753631_39?_encoding=UTF
8&psc=1&refRID=NKTZRWVVV3K4EY3T3MCT

36
https://www.google.com/search?sxsrf=ALeKk0231D44rCUTZTv
QQ6SBHwuhhN7vrw:1588006405424&source=univ&tbm=isch&
q=wire+compost+bin&sa=X&ved=2ahUKEwiT3MjtiInpAhVKa8
0KHTERDJMQsAR6BAgBEAE&biw=1328&bih=633

37 https://www.gardeners.com/buy/compost-aerator/33-367.html?utm_campaign=PLA&utm_medium=googleshopping&u
tm_source=google&SC=XNET0146&gclid=Cj0KCQjwhZr1BRC
LARIsALjRVQPAjFp4UVGriiEONYkXmtjBLfJz1II3jkl0YSkMq
8kZILJ0ChGdVA8aAh4CEALw_wcB

[38] My favorite pyramid bin is this one.
https://www.gardeners.com/how-to/video-pyramid-composter/8689.html?SC=XNET0348

There is even a video about it.
https://www.gardeners.com/how-to/video-pyramid-composter/8689.html?SC=XNET0348

https://www.gardeners.com/buy/evolution-pyramid-composter/8600227.html?utm_campaign=PLA&utm_medium=go

ogleshopping&utm_source=google&SC=XNET0146&gclid=Cj0K
CQjwka_1BRCPARIsAMlUmEqlwqAM9FL9Um_sxeP91SCCaU
tbKzjuVGhLDC5w_keAAz1zm71MQXAaAqMIEALw_wcB

39 My favorites:
Notice how low to the ground the stands are which makes them
sturdier.
https://www.amazon.com/Miracle-Gro-Dual-Chamber-Compost-
Tumbler/dp/B0785HCXB5/ref=zg_bs_3753631_9?_encoding=UT
F8&psc=1&refRID=NKTZRWVVV3K4EY3T3MCT

https://www.amazon.com/Dual-Body-Tumbling-Composter-
HOTFROG/dp/B01IFN972U/ref=zg_bs_3753631_24?_encoding=
UTF8&psc=1&refRID=NKTZRWVVV3K4EY3T3MCT

Also,
https://www.gardeners.com/buy/compost-
tumbler/8587257.html?irecsclick

[40] https://www.gardeners.com/buy/tumbling-composter-with-dual-
chambers/8590359.html?utm_campaign=PLA&utm_medium=goo
gleshopping&utm_source=google&SC=XNET0146&gclid=Cj0K
CQjwka_1BRCPARIsAMlUmEoKYOuzRHEPnN2KFTUiRLF8X
2a5eIcEw1CiLEqtbDf00A6ocnpKPxQaAooIEALw_wcB

41 https://www.gardeners.com/buy/dual-batch-compost-
tumbler/39-652.html

https://www.gardeners.com/buy/tumbling-composter-with-dual-
chambers/8590359.html?irecsclick

[42] Look at the top photo
https://nymag.com/strategist/article/best-compost-tumblers.html

https://www.cleanairgardening.com/spin-bin-tumbling-composter/

43 https://www.ippc.int/en/

https://en.wikipedia.org/wiki/IPPC

44 https://www.instructables.com/id/How-to-determine-if-a-wood-pallet-is-safe-for-use/

https://www.thebalancesmb.com/are-wood-pallets-safe-for-crafting-misinformation-abounds-2878158

https://www.1001pallets.com/pallet-safety/

[45] https://www.youtube.com/watch?v=qZDCUhtq7cg

[46]

https://www.goodhousekeeping.com/home/gardening/a20706669/how-to-build-compost-bin/

[47] https://www.gardeners.com/on/demandware.store/Sites-Gardeners-Site/default/Link-Product?pid=38-189&SC=XNET0350

[48] Pears, Pauline,.*Organic Book of Compost* Lifestyle Books, 2020.

49 https://www.veggiegardener.com/use-direct-composting-in-your-garden/

[50] https://youtu.be/WhUqyebBDeU

https://www.google.com/search?q=what+is+a+keyhole+garden?&sxsrf=ALeKk01kH09zrOMwYRg0W7OIW6TSzOAsQg:1588532014032&tbm=isch&source=iu&ictx=1&fir=L1dUpK0K-pUtbM%253A%252CtgFWp03fU-j_kM%252C%252Fg%252F11b8tw7vd3&vet=1&usg=AI4_-

kS0TPLiWvlXEvfxh9XwJLyHNpeKsg&sa=X&ved=2ahUKEwi7
iqTzrpjpAhXTQc0KHTpGAoUQ_B0wG3oECAoQAw&biw=134
4&bih=633#imgrc=u3VvAXDNYRzEpM

51 https://stonepierpress.org/gardeningnews/howtocompost

52https://greenactioncentre.ca/reduce-your-waste/compost-all-winter/

[53] http://www.homecompostingmadeeasy.com/composttea.html

[54] http://www.homecompostingmadeeasy.com/composttea.html

[55] *"Distinct differences exist between the microbial communities found in vermicomposts and composts. Hence, the nature of the microbial processes is quite different in vermicomposting and composting (Subler et al. 1998). The active phase of composting is the thermophilic stage. This stage is characterized by the thermophilic bacterial community where intensive decomposition takes place followed by a mesophilic maturation phase (Lazcano et al. 2008; Vivas et al. 2009)."*
file:///Users/cynthiamealy/Downloads/em9034%20(3).pdf

[56] **https://www.bhg.com/gardening/yard/garden-care/what-do-nitrogen-phosphorus-and-potassium-do/
https://www.sunset.com/garden/garden-basics/crash-course-fertilizers**

[57] You can find an incredible range of conflicting information on N-P-K content of vermicompost. It ranges from 0 nitrogen to "has more than compost does". In this guide, we are only citing the sources that reference scientific studies. The resources used in this guide for the science of vermicomposting can be found here:
https://www.ncbi.nlm.nih.gov/pmc/articles/PMC3725894/
http://www.carryoncomposting.com/416920205

http://compost.css.cornell.edu/worms/basics.html
https://www.stevespanglerscience.com/2013/06/14/the-science-behind-worms/

58

http://www.waldeneffect.org/blog/Worm_castings_vs._compost/

59

http://www.waldeneffect.org/blog/Worm_castings_vs._compost/

[60] https://www.tastefulgarden.com/Worm-Castings-d114.htm

[61] https://www.ncbi.nlm.nih.gov/pmc/articles/PMC3725894/

[62] https://www.ncbi.nlm.nih.gov/pmc/articles/PMC3725894/

[63] "Vermicomposting hastens the decomposition process by 2–5 times, thereby quickens the conversion of wastes into valuable biofertilizer and produces much more homogenous materials compared to thermophilic composting "(Bhatnagar and Palta 1996; Atiyeh et al. 2000a).
https://www.ncbi.nlm.nih.gov/pmc/articles/PMC3725894/

"Earthworms intestine contains a wide range of microorganisms, enzymes and hormones which aid in rapid decomposition of half-digested material transforming them into vermicompost in a short time (nearly 4–8 weeks) (Ghosh et al. 1999; Nagavallemma et al. 2004) compared to traditional composting process which takes advantage of microbes alone and thereby requires a prolonged period (nearly 20 weeks) for compost production (Bernal et al. 1998; Sánchez-Monedero et al. 2001)."
https://www.ncbi.nlm.nih.gov/pmc/articles/PMC3725894/

[64] https://naturesfootprint.com/community/articles/billions-of-microorganisms-in-the-worm-bin/
https://www.microbiologyresearch.org/docserver/fulltext/micro/31

/1/mic-31-1-
1.pdf?expires=1589316912&id=id&accname=guest&checksum=0
BC7C36D549A70B1CA06AA918B155497

[65] https://www.stevespanglerscience.com/2013/06/14/the-science-behind-worms/

As worms don't have lungs, they survive by breathing through their skin. They can suffocate if their skin dries out! A worm's body is made up of approximately 75% water, so if you maintain a moist environment, they won't have to work as hard to breathe and process their food. However, even though worms require water to breathe, they can't survive if submerged in water. In order to keep your worms alive and happy, you need to maintain ideal conditions, which means providing them with a moisture level of 75% (a few drops of water from a handful of bedding tightly squeezed), a temperature ranging between 15-25°C, a slightly acidic PH level, and plenty of oxygen."

[66] . https://www.tastefulgarden.com/Worm-Castings-d114.htm

[67] Holds 8-12,000 worms sohttps://www.dripworks.com/worm-factory?gclid=CjwKCAjwte71BRBCEiwAU_V9h3no6tiC7adyy_4GS0voZx2l0q2aZmGeUMliENhtiPntSD1I2JwUlhoC6wcQAvD_BwE

[68] https://sciencing.com/differences-between-earth-worms-and-compost-worms-12498654.html

https://www.kookaburrawormfarms.com.au/2018/01/25/5-things-didnt-know-compost-worms/

[69] http://compost.css.cornell.edu/worms/basics.html

[70] https://papillion-sanitation.com/worms-and-compost-the-science-of-verminculture/

[71] https://www.target.com/p/sterilite-18gal-storage-tote-brown/-/A-14757115

[72] https://www.dripworks.com/worm-factory?gclid=CjwKCAjwte71BRBCEiwAU_V9h3no6tiC7adyy_4GS0voZx2l0q2aZmGeUMliENhtiPntSD1I2JwUlhoC6wcQAvD_BwE

[73] Ebeling, Eric, Olenick, Patti and Hursh, Carl, Composting Basics: All the Skills and Tools You Need To Get Started, 2nd edition. Stackpole Books: Guilford, Connecticut, 2017.

Here is a good how-to resource as well:
https://www.tenthacrefarm.com/worm-bin-mistakes-problems/

http://compost.css.cornell.edu/worms/steps.html

[74] https://papillion-sanitation.com/worms-and-compost-the-science-of-verminculture/

[75] https://homeguides.sfgate.com/worms-eat-coffee-grounds-103941.html

https://homeguides.sfgate.com/worms-eat-coffee-grounds-103941.html

[76] You will find conflicting opinions about whether to feed your worms meat, dairy or oils/fat.

Those who say you can argue that worms will happily eat any organic material, including bone.
That is true, but I recommend not including these items for these reasons:

1) Your worms are not in the wild with all the space they need and freedom to move away when they want. They are confined to a bin.
2) Meat and dairy take a lot longer for the worms to eat than the rest of your food scraps.
As a result, you risk the meat and dairy rotting in your bin before the worms can finish it. This will kill your worms.
3) Meat and dairy attract wildlife (including rats and racoons) as well as pets to scrounge in your worm bin.
4) Oils and creamy or oily sauces will break down slower and will tend to soak the bedding resulting in the worms dying because they were unable to breathe.
Rinse off oily dressings from lettuces as well.

Read the story of Glenn in the comments of this page. It looked like his worms were fine, but they weren't, and he paid the price. http://www.compostjunkie.com/can-i-feed-my-worms-colored-newspaper.html

Here's what Uncle Jim has to say about what your worms can and can't eat:
https://unclejimswormfarm.com/foods-hurt-composting-worms/

Another resource for why not to include meat and dairy from Cornell
http://compost.css.cornell.edu/worms/basics.html

Personally, the only place I compost meat or dairy is in municipal compost.

[77] www.gardeners.com/how-to/worm-composting/5714.html

[78] http://compost.css.cornell.edu/worms/troubleshoot.html

[79] *https://wormfarmguru.com/worm-farm-problems/*

[80] https://unclejimswormfarm.com/how-to-get-rid-of-millipedes-

centipedes-and-mites-in-your-worm-bin/

[81]. https://homeguides.sfgate.com/problems-white-bugs-worm-farm-74148.html

[82] https://sustainableamerica.org/blog/compost-qa-troubleshooting-the-worm-bin/

[83] https://naturesfootprint.com/community/articles/bugs-creepy-crawlies-whats-in-my-worm-bin/

[84] https://naturesfootprint.com/community/articles/bugs-creepy-crawlies-whats-in-my-worm-bin/

[85] https://sustainableamerica.org/blog/compost-qa-troubleshooting-the-worm-bin/

[86] https://www.mentalfloss.com/article/49033/why-does-poop-stink

[87] Stan Wilson "*Humanure: Just do it*" Permaculture Design Magazine, No. 97. Fall:2015

[88] https://en.wikipedia.org/wiki/Night_soil

[89] Stan Wilson "*Humanure: Just do it*" Permaculture Design Magazine, No. 97. Fall:2015

[90] https://www.atlasobscura.com/articles/when-american-cities-were-full-of-crap There are also historical photographs and documented stories of the situation in large cities in this article.

[91] https://gardenerdy.com/how-to-build-composting-toilet

[92] https://en.wikipedia.org/wiki/Chemical_toilet

[93] https://www.mentalfloss.com/article/49033/why-does-poop-stink

[94] https://greywateraction.org/composting-toilets-faq/

[95] https://greywateraction.org/composting-toilets-faq/

[96] https://www.tomtur.com/composting-toilets-for-outbuildings/

[97] I note that the comments below this video include a person who says they use one bucket and have no problem whatsoever. Just remember, it's science. There are trade-offs. You can't get around the fact that you'd be putting much more liquid into the bucket that is supercharged with nitrogen. You will need more carbon to offset that (sawdust, wood shavings or peat moss) and that means changing over the bucket more often. https://www.youtube.com/watch?v=Jkk5pMJSv5E

[98] https://www.motherearthnews.com/homesteading-and-livestock/self-reliance/compost-toilet-ze0z1209zhar

https://home.howstuffworks.com/how-to-build-an-outhouse-with-a-composting-bucket-toilet3.htm

[99] https://www.weblife.org/humanure/chapter7_14.html

[100] https://www.fewresources.org/water-scarcity-issues-were-running-out-of-water.html
https://www.sciencedaily.com/terms/water_scarcity.htm

[101] Appendix 1: Science – Aerobic and Anaerobic Bacterial Activity
http://whatcom.wsu.edu/ag/compost/fundamentals/biology_anaerobic.htm
http://microbesinfo.com/2013/05/anaerobes-why-cant-anaerobic-organism-survive-in-presence-of-oxygen/

https://study.com/academy/lesson/aerobic-vs-anaerobic-bacteria-comparison-differences.html